ENGLISH POLITICS IN THE
THIRTEENTH CENTURY

British History in Perspective
General Editor: Jeremy Black

ENGLISH POLITICS
IN THE
THIRTEENTH CENTURY

MICHAEL PRESTWICH

Professor of History
University of Durham

MACMILLAN

First published 1990

Published by
MACMILLAN EDUCATION LTD
Houndmills, Basingstoke, Hampshire RG21 2XS
and London
Companies and representatives
throughout the world

Filmset by Wearside Tradespools,
Fulwell, Sunderland

Printed in Hong Kong

British Library Cataloguing in Publication Data
Prestwich, Michael
English politics in the thirteenth century. — (British
history in perspective. ISSN 0955–8322).
1. England. Politics, history
I. Title II. Series
320.942
ISBN 0–333–41433–0 (hardcover)
ISBN 0–333–41434–9 (paperback)

CONTENTS

PREFACE

THIS BOOK is intended to bring together recent ideas about the thirteenth century. The period is one which after some years of relative dormancy is now attracting a great deal of attention, as a new generation of historians question the conclusions of their predecessors. My debt to the various scholars working in this area is therefore a huge one, as I hope the notes reveal. Special thanks are due to Dr Peter Coss and Dr Simon Lloyd, for organising a very stimulating series of conferences for historians of the thirteenth century. I am grateful to the many students whom I have taught for this period; I owe them more than they realise. I would like to give warm thanks to Dr Robin Frame for reading an initial print-out of this book, and providing extremely helpful suggestions and corrections. My wife has provided invaluable help at all stages of the preparation of this book; without her support and assistance it could not have been written.

Durham, November 1989   MICHAEL PRESTWICH

INTRODUCTION

THE thirteenth century was an age when politics became distinctively English for the first time since 1066. From the Norman Conquest until John's reign, England had been a part of a wider political unit, of which Normandy was the heartland. By the second half of the twelfth century the king of England held most of western France, from Normandy to the Pyrenees. He ruled what is commonly called the Angevin Empire, though he was, of course, no emperor. The various lands that comprised this empire were not unified in the sense of sharing a common administrative or legal system, but because they had a single ruler it was inevitable that they would be politically interrelated. The complex events of the rebellion of 1173 against Henry II, which took place on both sides of the Channel, show that it would be quite wrong to think of the politics of that reign in purely English terms. In the thirteenth century, however, England became more insular. The loss of Normandy in 1204 was a crucial event, breaking the vitally important cross-Channel links that had bound England to the continental possessions of its rulers. It would be wrong to assume that England became isolated. One important qualification to make is that the British dimension became more important. Many major families had important interests in Ireland and Wales, which they expanded in the thirteenth century. Also, many who would today be termed Frenchmen sought to establish themselves in England. There were, however, never to be such close links in terms of landholding and family ties between England and its remaining continental possessions in Gascony, that part of south-western France which remained in English hands, as there had been with Normandy. For the first time since the Conquest of 1066, it makes sense to think about the English political system as a separate entity.

The grant by King John of Magna Carta in 1215 also marks a transformation. For the first time an attempt was made to resolve a political crisis by obtaining a wide-ranging set of concessions from the crown, concessions which aimed to impose legal limits on arbitrary royal actions, and which extended a measure of protection to all free men. In the short term the charter was a failure, hastening the onset of the civil war it was intended to prevent, but it showed what could be done. In the long term, Magna Carta in its revised form was to provide the essential bedrock of political liberties.

The change in the political structure of England that took place in this hundred years was immense. At the time of Magna Carta the political community was described as providing the common counsel of the realm. It was defined by Magna Carta in feudal terms, and consisted of the king's tenants-in-chief. The major barons were to be summoned individually, the remainder by the sheriff at a local level. It was envisaged that if it was necessary, twenty-five elected barons, with 'the community of the whole land', might compel the king to accept their judgements. A century later, the political nation was termed community of the realm. No longer was there any idea of an assembly of tenants-in-chief. Consultation now normally took place in parliament. A parliamentary peerage was developing, which was not defined in terms of any particular form of feudal tenure, and there was an elaborate system of representation, of shire, boroughs and lower clergy.

The reasons for such a transformation were diverse. Some historians would lay stress on the decline and decay of the old formal structures of tenurial feudalism. Others would emphasise the developing strength of the shire communities, and of the gentry society which provided their backbone. The impact of economic change was important: the decline in the crown's income from land, and the effects of inflation on the levels of expenditure, meant that the government was increasingly dependent on raising money by new means, in particular negotiated taxes. Methods had to be found for obtaining consent on a far wider scale than had been done in the past. At the same time there is a theoretical dimension. The influx of new ideas, particularly those derived from Roman law, may well have affected political practice, and the way in which men thought about the state and their relationship to it.

Politics in the thirteenth century, as at other periods, was about the ambitions of individuals, their personal friendships and, of course, their rivalries. It is possible to produce interpretations which largely neglect any questions of political ideals, and to see what took place in much more cynical terms of men seeking to better themselves. The competition for the lands of a great earldom, such as that of Pembroke, becomes in such an interpretation more important than abstract political ideals of government by counsel and consent. Private ambition and public good cannot be as easily disentangled as in more modern periods.

Political power lay ultimately with the crown, but it was not an absolute power. The crown was limited in a broad sense by a conception that the king should provide good lordship, and govern with good counsel. There was little consensus in the thirteenth century, however: the nature of royal authority was a matter of fierce debate. At a more practical level, an expansion of royal bureaucracy testified to an increase in royal power. More and more cases before royal courts, more and more business was conducted by royal sheriffs and other officials. At the same time, rights and privileges were jealously guarded against royal exploitation by those who possessed them. Property rights were protected by elaborate legal procedures, and inheritance customs were long settled and established. To obtain support, the crown needed to provide rewards in the form of land, but there was no inexhaustible supply of land readily available. To reward 'new men' was all too often to alienate established landowners.

It is not easy to appreciate the way in which the political system of a country such as England in the thirteenth century worked. There are no descriptions of the medieval equivalent of smoke-filled rooms where political questions were hotly debated. The political world was very small, dominated by small élite groups. The leading lay nobles possessed rank and landed wealth, and consequently influence, through birth. It was rare to find a man such as William the Marshal, who rose to the highest ranks of the aristocracy through his own ability. Personal likes and dislikes, good fortune in the marriage market, chance events on the tournament field, were all important in an age which knew faction but which did not know anything like the political parties of more modern periods. The upper echelons of the church provided another élite. The bishops achieved their status in a very different way from the lay magnates, but the criteria for appointment as a bishop were not necessarily those most appropriate to men of great influence in the councils of state. At a local level, in the county communities, the knights and gentry owed their influence in considerable measure to their lands and family position, while the stewards of the great lords played a very important role. The towns had their own élites of wealthy traders. The connections between the various groups in society were complex. There were what can be termed the vertical connections, provided by lordship, but there were also the horizontal connections provided by communities at different social levels, from that of the county down to the village.

It is not intended that this book should provide a narrative account of the political events of an exciting, vivid and complex period. However, a brief introduction to the events is necessary if discussion of the issues is not to be meaningless. King John, who came to the throne in 1199, is a man extraordinarily hard to assess. Early in his reign, in 1204, there was the disaster of the loss of Normandy: by the time of his death in 1216 the country was in the midst of civil war following baronial rebellion. Yet John was far from being an incompetent ruler. Many expedients he introduced set patterns for the crown to develop in the future, particularly under Edward I. The government bureaucracy, as witnessed by its record-keeping, became more efficient. New financial expedients were tried out. John's military ambitions, particularly his understandable desire to recover Normandy, entailed the imposition of considerable burdens on England. The king mismanaged the nobility, and handled the problems of the church badly. At the same time he showed an acute political awareness in his readiness to make concessions in return for support, forcing his opponents to develop a sophisticated programme. John's ambitions to recover his lost lands in France were abruptly halted in 1214 at the battle of Bouvines, fought by his allies. The road from Bouvines led to Runnymede and Magna Carta in 1215. That most celebrated document, in the context of John's reign, was no more than an abortive attempt to establish peace between the king and his baronial opponents. That it failed to do, and John died in 1216 in the midst of civil war.

The great charter of liberties was fundamental to the course of events for the rest of the century, not in the form that was agreed in 1215, but in the reissued and somewhat emasculated version of 1225. Magna Carta provided a ready-made programme for the political settlement of England during Henry III's minority, and the role of the papal legates in the initial reissues of 1216 and 1217 gave it a new stamp of authority. Henry's minority was in one sense remarkably successful, especially when compared to minorities in later periods. Civil war was ended, not started, and the power of the crown was maintained virtually intact, thanks to the work of men such as William the Marshal, earl of Pembroke, and Stephen Langton, archbishop of Canterbury. According to one interpretation, the minority gave the English baronage a taste of what could be achieved if government was conducted with their full participation. Another opinion, however, is that the inevitable development of faction in these years coloured the succeeding decades.

The years of Henry III's personal rule can appear as a series of crises, with the waves becoming steeper until they finally broke in 1258. Yet the period from 1234 to 1263 was peaceful in England, a very considerable achievement. There were, certainly, large problems and many arguments, but changes in the personnel of government were not the product of violence. At the outset the dominant figure was the justiciar, Hubert de Burgh. He fell from power in 1232, when his old rival, Peter des Roches, replaced him in a swift coup. The revolt of Richard the Marshal, earl of Pembroke, in 1234 resulted in the removal of des Roches. The successive departures of de Burgh and des Roches marked the breakup of the old factions which had dominated the minority. In the late 1230s and early 1240s the king's ministers tried to deal with the problems created by the king's ambitions to recover the lost lands in France, and with the legacy left by the minority. An important scheme for reform was proposed in 1244, but never put into effect. In 1253 the king sailed for Gascony, fearing invasion of his duchy from Castile. This provoked problems at home, and in the following years difficulties increased. There was a crisis in local government, troubles in Wales, and a ludicrously ambitious and costly scheme to acquire the Sicilian throne for the king's second son, Edmund.

The problems came to a head in 1258. The years of baronial reform and rebellion that lasted until 1265 were dominated by the controversial figure of Simon de Montfort. How far he was motivated by political idealism, how far by personal ambition of an opportunist character, will no doubt be long debated. The period of his dominance was notable for the range of solutions to the political difficulties of thirteenth-century England that were proposed, and the scale of the changes that were envisaged. At the Oxford parliament of 1258 a complex system was set up providing for the election of a council of fifteen which would control the king. Extensive inquiries took place at the county level,

6

and in 1259 the Provisions of Westminster set out a series of detailed legal measures. The baronial enterprise, however, was not united, and the king was able to re-establish his authority by 1261. The return from abroad of Simon de Montfort, earl of Leicester, in 1263 was followed by renewed political conflict. Earl Simon's refusal to accept the arbitration by the French king in the Mise of Amiens early in 1264 led to civil war, and the unexpected resounding baronial victory at Lewes. A new scheme of government, the *Forma Regiminis*, was put into effect, with three electors selecting a council of nine to govern the country. Montfort's triumph was shortlived. The young earl of Gloucester abandoned his cause, and the king's son, Edward, escaped from custody. In 1265 Montfort suffered defeat and death at the battle of Evesham.

The recovery of royal authority after Montfort's defeat at Evesham was not achieved by simply turning the clock back. Many of the lessons of the late 1250s and early 1260s were understood by Edward I, who came to the throne in 1272 (at a time when he was absent from the country on crusade). In his reign the political structure changed and developed further in response to new circumstances and ideas. The first half of the reign witnessed major achievements in legislation, with a succession of important statutes. Wales was conquered after campaigns in 1277 and 1282–3.

From the early 1290s the atmosphere changed, largely as a result of the heavy burden Edward I placed on the country in order to support his military ambitions. There was war with France, revolt in Wales and campaigns in Scotland. A major crisis occurred in 1297, when the clergy refused to pay a tax, the earls refused to perform military service overseas and there was widespread resentment of the demands of the crown. In the *Confirmatio Cartarum* concessions were made on various issues, notably taxation, and the king's right to purveyance, the compulsory purchase of foodstuffs. This was not enough. Arguments continued for the rest of the reign, and further concessions were made in the *Articuli super Cartas* of 1300. Many of the issues of 1297 were still smouldering in 1307, and the accession of the weak Edward

II did much to fan them into life. A new element in the political equation was provided by the king's Gascon favourite, Piers Gaveston. The extent of the favours granted to him represented a threat to the established nobility. The Ordinances of 1311 marked a further attempt to produce a major scheme to resolve the grievances of the nation. The consent of the baronage in parliament was now seen as essential in controlling the crown. The Ordinances can be regarded as the end of the historical chapter which opened with Magna Carta.

By no stretch of the imagination can this be regarded as a period neglected by historians, although there are surprising gaps in the historiography – above all, there has been no proper biographical study of Henry III, although one is now promised by D. A. Carpenter. The period was for long dominated by the works of Sir Maurice Powicke, notably *King Henry III and the Lord Edward*, and his study of the thirteenth century in the *Oxford History of England*. Powicke's books have been condemned by one recent writer, R. C. Stacey, for their air of 'vaguely Victorian constitutionalism'.[1] Powicke's was a magnificent achievement in many ways, but although he was exceptionally well read in the printed sources, he had no familiarity with the great range of unpublished material in the Public Record Office. He had a certain distaste, or so it seems, for the details of financial history, and his splendid phrases can obfuscate as much as illuminate. It is unfair, however, to level too much criticism at works published in the late 1940s and early 1950s: it is inevitable that, in many areas, what Powicke wrote should need to be updated. Much has been written since he wrote.

In particular, there has been a great deal of debate about the nature of parliament: was it, as H. G. Richardson and G. O. Sayles have argued with total commitment and consistency since the 1920s, first and foremost a legal body, the essence of which was the king and his council hearing cases and petitions; or was it as many historians suggest, a body less capable of precise definition, possessing a remarkably broad range of capabilities, and including on some occasions a very significant representative element?[2] Local administration has been the subject of much work: the nature of the sheriff's office, and of the pressures put on that hard-worked official by the central administration, and in particular the exchequer, has been studied in detail. The character of the county community is still a matter for argument, with contradictory impressions gained by political and legal historians. Taxation has been studied, both from the point of view of financial history, and also from the constitutional aspect. There has been debate about what kind of obligation the king's subjects were under to make grants of taxation. One important suggestion is that in this period ideas drawn from Roman law had a significant impact on English practice. An area that has seen recent advances is the analysis of the political importance of the aliens in Henry iii's court, the Savoyards who came to England in the wake of the queen, and the Poitevin half-brothers of the king and their hangers-on. Where the crisis of 1258 was once seen in terms of a country-wide revulsion at the crown's policies, recent arguments see divisions between the alien factions in the court as being of prime importance.

The reign of Edward i has not, perhaps, undergone as startling a revision as that of Henry iii, but research since Powicke wrote has laid much greater stress on the impact upon the country of the king's wars.[3] Interpretations of the king's policies towards his earls have taken a much more cynical turn, and the crisis of 1297 has undergone detailed analysis. The topic of military service is another which has received fresh attention. Was it the case that this period saw the collapse of feudal techniques of military recruitment, and that a military revolution took place with pay serving as the catalyst for change? This book does not enter far into the reign of Edward ii, but there the revolution in historical thinking has perhaps been even more startling than for the reigns of Henry iii and Edward i. The old orthodoxies that saw the central struggle in terms of a conflict between household administration, and government through the great offices of state, the chancery and the exchequer, have been abandoned in favour of an interpretation that lays much more stress on personal ambitions and rivalries.[4]

The approach adopted here is analytical rather than chronological. It is hoped that a study of certain specific themes may help to illuminate some of the attitudes and practices of an involved period. The crown, nobility and county communities are each examined, as is the church. Each had a distinctive part to play in the political system. Three particular issues are looked at: the hostility that existed towards foreigners, the problems posed by military service and the question of taxation. This is, of course, a limited and perhaps idiosyncratic selection, but each bears on different aspects of the political processes of the period. They all help to demonstrate the way in which the governing élites responded to the many pressures on them. The concept of the community of the realm is a difficult one, which could not be translated into the English of the thirteenth century, and is not easy to express in that of the twentieth. The relationship between it and the developing institution of parliament provides the final theme for this book.

1

KINGSHIP

IT IS HARD, in these days of an emasculated constitutional monarchy, to comprehend the full scale of the power and authority of a medieval king. The personality of a ruler did much to condition the nature of politics in his reign. John, complex, tricky and devious; Henry III, a curious mixture of piety, arrogance and weakness; Edward I, strong, autocratic, at times principled and at times not; Edward II, weak and almost completely lacking in kingly qualities – these men were at the centre of the political developments and disputes of their reigns. It was not, indeed, until 1308 that the doctrine separating the person of the king from the institution of the crown was clearly set out. Yet politics was not simply a matter of personalities. There were important questions to be asked, and answered, about the nature of monarchical authority. There were very different views of the office of a king, and those differences lay at the heart of much political conflict. These views could be categorised in simple terms of absolutism and constitutionalism, but there are dangers in attempting to apply to the past concepts which were unfamiliar to contemporaries. A further problem is that while there were some very sophisticated ideas in some circles, it is far from clear how widely they were disseminated or understood, and therefore how relevant they were to practical politics.

The *Song of Lewes*, written by a fierce propagandist of the baronial cause in 1264, set out two opposing views of monarchy with the clear, exaggerated lines of a cartoonist.[1] The royal view was that the king wished to be free, and his supporters urged that he should be. If he could not do as he wished, he would no longer be a king. It was not up to the magnates to decide who should be appointed to earldoms, or to the custody of castles, or to be judges. The king should be able to choose whoever he wished to be his treasurer and chancellor, and he should be able to select councillors of any nationality. The barons should not interfere in the king's actions. The command of the prince should have the force of law, and all should be bound to obey his decisions. Earls had similar powers over their own men, as did barons, knights and free men: why should the king be placed in an inferior position to them? According to this argument, the king should be like his predecessors, who ruled according to their will.

The alternative case was set out at length: it was the one with which the author sympathised. Ultimate authority lay with God, and it was a monarch's duty to God to rule according to the law. If a king ruled justly, then he would, of course, be honoured. If a king lacked wisdom, however, he should not rely on his judgement alone, but should be counselled by the community of the realm, who would be familiar with the laws. Native-born men would be in the best position to act as councillors and helpers to the king; they would have knowledge passed down by their fathers, and would have the greatest concern for the kingdom. That which permitted fools to rule unwisely should not be called liberty; true liberty exists within the boundaries of the law. The king should not prefer his private interests to those of the community; his task was to protect his subjects, and to work for the salvation of the realm. If he asked aid from his people, he should inform them of his plans. A king should govern his kingdom together with his nobles, relying on native-born men, not foreigners. The essence of the argument was that the king should rule according to natural, or

12

divine, law, and that if he failed to do so it was the task of the English magnates to advise and correct him.

These views set out in the *Songs of Lewes* were in part the product of the particular crisis of the Barons' Wars. Some of the arguments reflected immediate concerns, such as the emphasis on native-born advisors. The general arguments, however, were more broadly based. The author, probably a friar, was well aware of scholastic debate about the nature of the state. The *Song* no doubt set principles one against another with much greater clarity than was really warranted, and it can be argued that there was more disagreement over the interpretation of principles of government than over the principles themselves. The contrasts set out by the author are, however, very useful. The idea that a king might rule according to his will was a well-established one for the Angevin monarchy. The king's will, and also his ill will, was a powerful weapon in the hands of a man such as King John. There might be considerable problems in established custom: men might prefer a case to be determined by the exercise of the king's will, untramelled by past precedent and perhaps in consequence more equitable. At the same time, the king's ill will, or *malvolentia*, was almost tangible, and was much feared. Those who incurred John's ill will, for whatever offence, might have to pay dearly to regain his good opinion of them. Robert de Vaux, for example, was charged 750 marks to obtain the king's goodwill (*benevolentia*) in 1210.[2] It was expedient that the king should be able to act according to his will on occasion, but there was a striking contrast between the king as upholder of the due process of law, and the king who could override the law at his own whim, in a manner not permitted to any of his subjects.

At the other end of the thirteenth century, Edward I did not express his power to act according to his will as blatantly as had his grandfather John. His instructions to the exchequer when a group of magnates refused to go to Gascony were clear enough, however: the debts that they owed to the crown were to be collected, their lands were to be harshly distrained, they were to be offered no favours but were to be oppressed by all possible means.[3] In 1297 it was by the king's will that, as a result of their refusal to grant a tax, the clergy were excluded from the king's protection and effectively outlawed. The bishop of Llandaff continued his resistance far longer than most clerics, and the exchequer was told that 'it is our will that of the said temporalities [of the bishopric of Llandaff] . . . up to a quarter should be collected for our use for this disobedience'.[4] When Henry Keighley was imprisoned for presenting to Edward a parliamentary bill critical of the king, there was no question of any trial – he was simply to be held in custody at the king's will until there was evidence that he repented of what he had done.[5]

The argument that the king had the right to appoint whomsoever he wished as his officials was put forward by Henry III in 1248, when the king claimed that his barons were refusing him the right which every head of a household had to appoint or remove servants. In 1301 Edward I reacted similarly to criticism of his corrupt treasurer, Walter Langton, arguing that his critics were trying to reduce him to a servile level, denying him rights they possessed themselves. When the royal household played a central role in the government of the country, it was hard to draw the distinction, obvious today, between the king's domestic servants and the officers of state. The contrast between the freedom allowed to his subjects and the limitations with which the monarchy was threatened was also pointed out by Edward I in 1297, when attempts were made to prevent him imposing a compulsory seizure of wool: 'It seems to us that we should be as free as any man to buy wool in our own country.'[6] The idea of the king acting as if he had the authority of the head of a household over his entire realm was not one set out by scholarly authorities, but it was nevertheless a powerful concept with deep roots in the past.

Henry III had another weapon in his armoury of ideas about the nature of royal authority. He saw himself as God's vicar on earth, with an obligation to look after the affairs of his subjects. The idea that rulers had some divine authority was not new, and was indeed to some extent at variance with the new ideas of the thirteenth century about the proper relationship of church and state. For the canon lawyers of the period, papal power was superior to royal, and would ensure that kings observed what was thought to be natural law. Henry nevertheless did much to establish the theocratic, or sacral, elements of his kingship in order to boost his authority. He had the *Laudes regiae*, hymns in honour of the crown, sung frequently. It seems very probable that it was in his reign that the practice of touching for the king's evil began, making use of the alleged healing abilities of monarchy. It is likely that in doing this Henry was emulating his great rival, Louis IX of France. He certainly followed Louis's example in his church building, rebuilding Westminster Abbey as a centre for the English monarchy, a church for royal coronations and burials. His son Edward I was not a man of such sophisticated personal piety, but he continued with the touching of the sick, and the chapel of St Stephen's, Westminster, was clearly designed as an English rival to the French Sainte Chapelle. The spiritual authority of the crown was ill defined, but it was an important attribute of monarchy, and an element which quite clearly distinguished the crown from the type of authority exercised by such secular lords as earls and barons. One of Edward I's proclamations began by arguing that the king had received the government of the realm by divine ordinance.[7]

The *Song of Lewes* included little explicitly about feudal concepts of lordship as they might apply to the monarchy. The obligations that resulted from the fealty and homage performed to the king by his tenants-in-chief were still significant in the thirteenth century, even though some aspects of the feudal relationship no longer had the force they had possessed in the eleventh century. It is striking that when Edward I was faced with determined opposition in 1297 to his plans for a campaign in Flanders, he demanded that his subjects should do their duty, as good and loyal men should and were obliged to do to their liege lord. This was the language of feudalism.[8] Edward also made much of his feudal rights in his attempts to extend his rule. It was Llywelyn ap Gruffudd's refusal to appear to do homage that contributed to the outbreak of the first Welsh war in 1277, and in Scotland Edward's determination to establish his rights to feudal overlordship led him into a succession of increasingly frustrating campaigns. Feudal service may have been becoming obsolete, but the fundamental concepts of feudal lordship were very much alive.

In 1258 the pope was informed that Henry III's half-brothers had suggested to him that a prince should not be subject to the law, a clear reference to the Roman law tag *quod principi placuit legem habet vigorem* ('what pleases the prince has the force of law'). This concept in proper hands was not a recipe for absolutism, but it could easily be misunderstood in this way.[9] It was a different Roman law doctrine, that of necessity, which provided the greatest support to a monarch. The central purpose of a ruler was, according to the ideas developed by civil and canon lawyers, the preservation of the state. In the twelfth century canonists had established the principle that in times of emergency, necessity might override the law. The emergency had to be one that threatened the well-being of the whole people: to defend the common good a ruler could demand the assistance of all. The doctrine was set out very clearly in the thirteenth century by Thomas Aquinas: 'Where princes do not possess sufficient means to provide against hostile attack ... it is just that citizens should contribute what is necessary to promote the common interest'.[10] It is not always easy to determine whether a king was appealing to this doctrine of necessity, or merely making a factual statement of the current situation. Necessity was very specifically mentioned in Richard I's reign, in connection with the need to pay the king's ransom, even though this was a feudal obligation *par excellence*. In 1205 John's summons to a great council to discuss both his grave and important affairs, and the common utility of the realm, and his stress on the prospect of foreign invasion when introducing a novel scheme for military service, both suggest at the least a full awareness of the principles drawn from Roman law. The same is true of the king's justification for the tax of a thirteenth imposed in 1207 'for the defence of the realm and the recovery of our right'.[11] In Henry III's reign, Stephen Langton appealed to the notion of necessity very explicitly, and in 1254 aid was sought on the grounds of the necessity facing the king. By Edward I's reign, however, necessity was not appealed to on any scale. The argument could aptly have been used in 1297, but the king and his officials did not use it in their dealings with the earls, and did little more than allude to it in approaching the clergy.

There was, therefore, a substantial body of ideas lending support to the monarchy. At the same time, as the author of the *Song of Lewes* emphasised, there were other concepts. The notion of the theocratic king was hardly welcome to all churchmen. While Bishop Grosseteste accepted the fact that unction at the coronation endowed a king with an authority not permitted to the unanointed, he was quick to remind Henry III of the fate of Uzziah king of Judah, struck down with leprosy for taking on the office of a priest.[12] There was, by the thirteenth century, a well-developed papal theory permitting the papacy to depose inadequate rulers. Innocent IV had no compunction about depriving Sancho IV of Portugal of all practical power in 1245, basing his action on the plenitude of power which the pope claimed to possess as vicar of Christ. This Portuguese example could well have been a precedent in Simon de Montfort's mind: he surely regarded Henry III as a *rex inutilis* (an inadequate king), just as Innocent IV regarded Sancho.[13] On a less serious note, Edward I was reminded, when about to enter the city of Oxford, about the curse which St Frideswide, a virtuous Anglo-Saxon saint, had laid on kings who approached her shrine. He duly declined to enter the city. The church was not always the support for the monarchy that kings wished.

Feudal law and the ideas that underlay it may have given the king great authority, but at the same time he had obligations. The implication of a feudal relationship was that the tenant should receive protection from his lord in return for the services he provided, services which included the right and duty to offer counsel. It was possible for feudal law to be adapted in such a way as to render a king virtually powerless in the face of his united vassals, as events in the thirteenth-century kingdom of Jerusalem illustrated. There it was not possible for the king to proceed against any of his vassals without obtaining a judgement of the Haute Cour. In England there were considerable constraints imposed by feudal custom on the king. He was, for example, only entitled to taxation by right for three purposes: his own ransom, the knighting of his eldest son, and the marriage of his eldest daughter. While he could summon the feudal host when he wished, the period of service to which he was entitled was limited to 40 days. The question of how far feudal custom obliged the king to take the advice of his tenants-in-chief is, however, a difficult one. It used to be considered that demands that the king govern with the assistance of his 'natural councillors' was a reference to this concept, but in practice in this period the phrase meant no more than 'native-born councillors', as opposed to aliens. In 1234 the archbishop-elect of Canterbury protested at the way in which the native-born men of the realm had been driven from the royal court.[14] Magna Carta, however, had laid down the composition of the common counsel of the realm in feudal terms of those who held directly from the king, and there can be little doubt that there was a sense in which the baronage felt that their voice should be heard in royal councils. It was also the case that kings often thought it necessary to obtain the consent of the magnates and on occasion others. King John stressed the consent he obtained, as for example to the tax of a thirteenth in 1207, or to military arrangements in 1205. There is, however, evidence of his consulting the magnates in lawsuits on only three occasions, in contrast to at least nine under Henry III in the ten years 1228–38.[15]

The idea of a contract between the king and his most important subjects was put in a pseudo-historical context in a curious tract written in about 1290, the *Mirror of Justices*. Here it was explained that the origin of political society in England was the decision of forty original Anglo-Saxon chieftains who settled in England to elect a king, who was made to swear to maintain the Christian faith, to rule by law and to accept the law himself. He should have companions (counts or earls) in parliament to hear cases about wrongs he or his officials might commit. There is no suggestion that the king should consult anyone below the rank of earl. The tract did not have a wide circulation, and its ideas were not picked up on any scale by others, but the ideas put forward are interesting, suggesting as they do that political society was founded upon an original contract. The *Mirror* considered that the king should have no peers in the land, but there were much more radical views about. One thirteenth-century formulary explained that 'the community of subjects is mightier than the dignity or lordship of any king set over his subjects'.[16]

Roman law, which at first sight lends support to autocratic ideas of kingship, provided some theoretical checks on the crown. The doctrine of necessity did not permit a ruler to do as he chose. There was the question of who could declare that a necessity existed. The obvious answer was the king himself, but in 1254 Henry III's claim for aid on grounds of necessity backfired when it became clear that the threat of an invasion of Gascony from Castile was non-existent, and that there was no true emergency at all. More important limitations on royal authority were derived from the principle of consultation contained in Roman law. The doctrine of *quod omnes tangit* ('what touches all should be approved by all'), can be seen as binding rulers to obtain the consent of their subjects for their actions, and much has been made of it by some historians. It can be found in both civil and canon law, and was certainly known in England in the mid-thirteenth century. Allusion was made to it in a scheme for government drawn up in 1244, and Matthew Paris referred to it under the year 1251. The most celebrated use of it came when the clergy were summoned to parliament in 1295: Stubbs saw it as being 'transmuted by Edward from a mere legal maxim into a great political and constitutional principle'.[17] Yet it was used only once, and then merely in summoning the clergy, the group which might be expected to be most familiar with such legal tags. Its force should not be exaggerated. *Quod omnes tangit* was not used by the crown's opponents, save to a limited extent in 1244, as a means of compelling the crown to accept principles of counsel and consent. It was not used by the author of the *Song of Lewes*, and there is no evidence that the king, or anyone else, regarded it as a binding political principle. Edward ɪ's opponents in 1297 did not employ it in their arguments against the king's attempts at what they saw as arbitrary taxation, even though it would seem ideally suited to their purpose.

As the evidence of Edward ɪ's use of *quod omnes tangit* shows, the crown was ready to accept principles of consultation and consent. Early in his reign Edward told the pope that he could not act without consultation, and in 1302 he claimed that he was 'allied to the good people of our realm in such manner' that he required their counsel. It was useful on occasion for the king to hide behind his subjects in this way, and such statements should be, and no doubt were, taken with a pinch of salt. Edward was well aware of the importance of carrying his subjects with him, as when he obtained full consent for his Scottish campaign of 1298, but he was equally capable of persisting in his plans in face of virtually unanimous hostility, as in his expedition to Flanders in 1297.

The *Song of Lewes* emphasised, in the justification of the opposition case, the importance of the king being subject to the law. This was a well-established idea, for all that it apparently conflicted with *quod principi placuit legem habet vigorem*. The precise form of the coronation oath sworn prior to the accession of Edward ɪɪ is not known, but it is evident that a promise to adhere to the laws of the Confessor was an element in it. A version of the Laws of Edward the Confessor found in a legal collection put together at the start of the thirteenth century contained a number of additions: the unknown author of these hoped to give them authority by interpolating them into more genuine material. It was stressed that law, not will, should be the basis of rule. The role of the magnates was vital: the king must act according to their advice and judgement. Law was made by the authority of the ruler with the counsel of the magnates. The king was also bound to preserve the rights of the crown, a doctrine which hinted at the separation of the institution of monarchy from the person of the king, and which led to the idea that crown lands must remain in royal hands, and could not be granted out.

Ideas about the crown were developed further in the thirteenth-century legal treatise which goes under the name of Bracton, and which was probably written either by the justice William Raleigh, or by one of his entourage, in the 1220s or 1230s. At one point it is suggested that God alone could punish a wrongful king. No one person was superior to the king, but the king and magnates together had the authority to change and make laws, something which the king alone could not do. In a celebrated *addicio*, an addition to the treatise, possibly written later and not necessarily by the same author, the arguments were taken further. God and the law were superior to the king, and the court of earls and barons was there to restrain the king if he should act contrary to the law. Some of the arguments were odd ones. The earls are called *comites*, or fellows of the king. Anyone who has a fellow has a master, and it was the duty of the earls to bridle the king if he proved to be unbridled. There has been much discussion of this section of the treatise, and it can be argued that it is far from being as radical as it superficially appears to be. Clearly, however, for all that it is possible to read it in different ways, it stands firmly counter to any autocratic ideas.[18]

There was little disagreement over the fundamental point that the king should maintain and preserve the law, and that he had a duty to God to do so. The problem was how to ensure that he did this: from one point of view the king had no superior to whom he might be answerable, but from another, the magnates had the prime responsibility. What means were available to them? Different approaches reflected both different aspects of thoughts about kingship, and different political circumstances. One method was to define the law, and to trust that the king would obey it. The other was to ensure that he was properly advised, by imposing on him the counsel of an appropriate body of men.

Magna Carta was by any standards a quite exceptional document. The idea that the king should be under, not above, the law was central to the Charter, although in a sense, as the document took the form of a grant by the king, his superiority was still evident. The crown's freedom of action was limited in many ways by the Charter. Reliefs, the feudal inheritance payment, were set at fixed levels of £100 for a barony and £5 for a knight's fee. Aids could only be levied without consent to pay for the ransoming of the king, the knighting of his eldest son, or the marriage of his eldest daughter. Nothing more than the customary level of service was to be demanded from knights' fees. Royal officials were not to take corn or other goods without paying cash, or agreeing terms for payment. A number of clauses laid down rules intended to make justice properly available, and the celebrated clause 39 promised that no action would be taken against any free man without 'the lawful judgement of his peers or by the law of the land'.

The final section of Magna Carta attempted to guarantee that the king would adhere to the law. It was laid down that if the king, or any of his officials, went against the terms agreed, the issue could then be put to four out of a committee of twenty-five barons, who could demand that a remedy be provided. In the event of the king or his justiciar failing to do this, then as a last resort the twenty-five, along with the community of the land, might force compliance by distraining the king's castles, lands and possessions. This was not, as has sometimes been thought, a legalisation of rebellion. It was simply the only route available to compel the king to accept judgements which went against him. The scheme proved unworkable in the circumstances of 1215. It was unacceptable to John, and did not provide his opponents with sufficient weapons. The Charter failed to prevent the drift into civil war. When it was reissued during Henry III's minority, this section was omitted, and the scheme it contained was never revived.[19]

Most clauses of Magna Carta were retained in the reissues of 1216, 1217 and 1225, and the document acquired a status which meant that its terms could never be lightly overridden by any king. In 1217 the Charter of the Forest was issued. The king had extensive arbitrary rights over the wide tracts of land allocated as royal forest. Arrangements were made for the boundaries to be checked, so that recent afforestation could be cancelled. Abuses were dealt with, and checks were imposed on extortion by officials.

Demands for the reissue of the charters were a regular feature of political crisis: Magna Carta was to some extent seen as a panacea. The 1225 version was confirmed in 1237, and again in 1253. In 1275 Edward I ordered that the provisions of Magna Carta should be adhered to, and the document was again reissued in 1297, and in 1300. By the end of the century the Charter, along with the Charter of the Forest, was no longer the solution to political problems that men hoped it would be, and there were to be no further reissues.

The various schemes proposed for controlling the crown in Henry III's reign took a very different form from that of 1215. One recurrent idea was that a council, or councillors, should be imposed on the king, so as to ensure that he was guided by men of wise and sensible views. This was a product of the years of the minority, when the country had indeed been governed by a council dominated by magnates with a good deal of success. There was as yet no clear definition of the membership of the council: it usually contained a magnate element, both lay and ecclesiastical, and an official element, consisting of men with administrative and legal expertise. By the 1230s it is clear that the king's councillors swore a special oath. In the aftermath of Richard the Marshal's rebellion, in 1234, various men were removed from the council, and others added to it. In 1236 a council of twelve was named, the members of which swore to give the king faithful counsel. In 1244 the scheme, known as the Paper Constitution, which was never put into effect, allowed for four councillors to be elected by common consent. At least two were always to be present, and they could not be removed from the council without the same consent that had seen them appointed.

There was hope during the years of Henry III's personal rule that effective reform might be achieved by appointing respected men to the positions of justiciar and chancellor. No justiciar had been appointed after Stephen Segrave briefly replaced Hubert de Burgh in 1234, and control of the seal was taken away from the chancellor, Ralph Neville, in 1238. Henry relied instead on household officials, many of them Poitevins or Savoyards. The Paper Constitution of 1244 required that a chancellor and a justiciar should be 'elected by all'. Neville had refused to authorise various grants in 1232, notably those to Peter des Rivaux, and had claimed that he had been given the seal by common counsel, and so could not be removed without common assent. His career provided an excellent example of the type of official that was envisaged in 1244.[20]

When the major crisis of Henry's reign broke in 1258, a central element of the solution propounded by the king's opponents was the creation of a permanent council of fifteen, elected by a complex mechanism by twenty-four barons, twelve of them royalists, and twelve baronial supporters. This body operated for some time, but the scheme was hardly viable in view of the king's hostility to it. The reformers made no change to the office of chancellor, but a baronial justiciar was appointed in the form of Hugh Bigod: he was replaced by Hugh Despenser in 1260. By early 1261 the council had collapsed, and in June Despenser was dismissed. Henry III argued in a set of grievances against the council that 'It seems to some that if the king proposes something better than they, that his opinion should prevail, and that they should not do something less good than he proposes'. In reply, the council had to agree that when the king talked sense, he should be listened to. It was not intended to take all dignity, regality or power from him, and reasonable royal commands should be obeyed: the implication was that Henry was rarely reasonable.[21]

In 1264 the *Forma Regiminis* (the scheme of government put together after Simon de Montfort's triumph at Lewes) allowed for a council of nine, nominated by three electors, one of whom, naturally, was Montfort himself. The king was no more than a puppet, allowed to retain his royal title, but not permitted to exercise any authority. The scheme did not work for long. One of the electors, the young earl of Gloucester, quarrelled with Montfort, and in practice the regime became increasingly autocratic. Montfort's decision to investigate the nature of the powers he could claim in his hereditary capacity as Steward of England shows that he considered that he needed greater authority than the *Forma Regiminis* allowed him. The defeat of Earl Simon in 1265 at Evesham spelled an end for half a century to the idea of imposing councillors on the king as a means of controlling him.

It would be very wrong to give the impression that there was a continual conflict during the thirteenth century between the crown and its critics, with one crisis relentlessly succeeding another in a crescendo. The problems that faced Henry III were intermittent, and it was not until 1263 that civil war broke out. The first half of Edward I's reign saw no serious threats to royal authority. With effective kingship some of the reforming policies of the late 1250s were put into effect, particularly those concerned with law and local government. Themes can be traced in Edward's legislation which go back to the Provisions of Westminster of 1259. The inquiry which yielded the Hundred Rolls of 1274–5 echoed the inquest conducted by the justiciar, Hugh Bigod, in 1258–9. It was possible for the crown to mount the massive *quo warranto* inquiries into the rights of jurisdiction exercised by magnates and others without provoking a storm of hostility. In the course of the hearings royal lawyers emphasised the theory that all rights of jurisdiction were ultimately derived from the crown: magnate claims to exercise rights simply because they and their ancestors had done so from time immemorial were firmly challenged.[22]

It was not until 1297 that the question of imposing limitations upon Edward I had to be considered. The need to pay for war in Wales and France had forced the king into what were widely considered to be improper measures. Taxes, both direct and indirect, and levies of foodstuffs, or prises, had been imposed without proper consent. There was now no thought of imposing councillors on the king. The events of the 1260s had discredited such methods, which would in any case have been unlikely to have been accepted by so strong-willed and obstinate a man as Edward I. The reissue of the Charters was a central demand, and it has to be suspected that men thought much more would be achieved by this than was in fact the case. It seems that it was hoped to add new clauses to Magna Carta which would deal with the specific problems that had arisen in the 1290s, but in the resolution of the crisis these new clauses made up a separate document, the *Confirmatio Cartarum*. Common assent of all the realm was now required for taxation and other imposi-tions. Sanctions were introduced in order to ensure adher-ence to the terms of the Charters, taking the form of sentences of excommunication against all who might break those terms. Such steps lacked real force, but even so, Edward considered it worth obtaining from the pope in 1305 formal release from his promises. The concessions made by the king in the *Articuli super Cartas* of 1300, covering a range of specific matters, were not accompanied by any new form of sanction against the king: instead, Edward had a clause included which reserved his royal rights. The difficulties involved in dealing with so strong a king as Edward were illustrated in 1301, when, according to one chronicler, the members of a committee appointed to decide if the requests made in parliament were compatible with the preservation of the crown refused to act.[23]

The issues raised in 1297 and 1300 were far from resolved at the end of Edward I's reign. The unfortunate Edward II received a legacy from his father of heavy debts probably totalling £200,000, and of unresolved political problems. To these he added the issue of his favourite Piers Gaveston, who was loathed by the English magnates. It proved possible to use the king's affection for Gaveston as a political weapon: in 1309 concessions were extracted from Edward in return for permitting Gaveston to return from exile. That did not solve the problems. Financial pressure was put on the king by refusing to allow him to collect taxes, and this forced Edward II in 1310 to agree to the appointment of a reforming commission of twenty-one Ordainers.

The Ordainers were not councillors: their task was to work out the specific measures that were needed. It is striking that whereas in 1215 Magna Carta had provided new statements of law, now in 1311 the Ordinances concentrated on providing checks on administrative malpractice and on controlling royal patronage. In political terms there was a significant new development, for on a number of important matters the document demanded the consent of the baronage in parliament. Parliament as such had not been mentioned in 1297: this was the first time that the institution had been specified in this way. The Ordinances were to be regarded as a most serious check on the crown: they were to be repealed in the Statute of York of 1322 because of the way in which royal power and the estate of the crown had been limited and confined.

There were very different ideas about the nature of royal authority in the thirteenth century. Although there was no pure absolutist theory, the idea that the king had full authority within his kingdom, and that he was only subject to God and perhaps the pope, was an attractive one for those who saw their fortunes indissolubly linked to the royal court. If ideas from Roman law were added, suggesting that the king was above the law, and that he had almost unlimited rights in time of necessity, that provided a powerful armoury. Louis IX, in the Mise of Amiens of 1264, declared that Henry III should have 'full power and free authority in his kingdom'.[24] There were, however, good arguments showing that kings had an obligation to rule justly, and to do so with proper consultation. Depositions of kings by the papacy showed that lay rulers were vulnerable. In practical terms, attempts were made to control the crown by means of changes in the law, and by imposing councillors and officials on an unwilling king. Good government was hard to achieve by such means, as the reigns of John and Henry III showed. Under Edward I, the years of success before the outbreak of the war with France in 1294 showed what could be achieved by a king when his rule was broadly in sympathy with his subjects' aspirations. With the pressures of war in Edward's later years, however, and the ineffective rule of his son Edward II, it became clear once again that the problems of defining the extent and nature of royal authority had not been fully solved.

2

THE ARISTOCRACY

MEDIEVAL BARONS have traditionally received a bad press.
Bishop Stubbs, writing in the nineteenth century, found little
good to say about those of the thirteenth century. The earls
of Gloucester, 'neither of them gifted with genius, try to play
a part that genius only could make successful'. 'Bohun and
Bigod, the heroes of 1297, are but degenerate sons of mighty
fathers'. He was prepared to allow 'constructive genius' to
Simon de Montfort, but even so, 'the great merit of his
statesmanship is adaptive rather than originative'. Such
judgements are dangerous, and K. B. McFarlane was fully
justified when he suggested in 1965 that a more sympathetic
understanding of the medieval nobility was required.[1]

The nobles dominated politics. It could hardly have been
otherwise: these were the men of wealth and status in a
hierarchical society. Seven out of the twenty-five barons of
Magna Carta were earls. It is hard to imagine that, able as he
was, Simon de Montfort would have been acceptable as a
leader of the movement against Henry III had he not been
earl of Leicester. In 1297 it was the earls of Norfolk and
Hereford who headed opposition to Edward I.

Contemporary chroniclers and modern historians alike
write of 'the baronage', a term which disguises the extent of
social gradation within the ranks of the aristocracy. At the
head of the hierarchy were the earls, numbering less than a
dozen for most of the thirteenth century. Their estates would

normally stretch far beyond the single county from which their title was derived. The earls of Gloucester, for example, held lands extending right across southern England, as well as major lordships in south Wales and Ireland.

Below the earls were the barons. These are best, if unhelpfully, defined as men who held baronies. Their number may have extended to about 200 families at the most. In 1299, eleven earls and seventy-nine barons were individually summoned to parliament, a figure which gives an impression of the size of the political élite. Below the barons were the knights. Although they were considered to be noble, and were addressed as *sire*, they were not part of the aristocracy like the earls and barons.

Great changes took place within the highest rank of the aristocracy, that of the earls, in the thirteenth century. The 1240s was a startling decade, with no less than ten earls dying. Major shifts took place as old families failed and new ones came to take their place. Straightforward descent from father to son through the thirteenth century was rare: the Warenne earls of Surrey provide one of the few examples of it, as do the insignificant earls of Oxford. The list of earldoms which, for one reason or another, failed or fell into abeyance between 1216 and 1311 is an impressive one: Aumale, Cornwall, Chester, Derby, Devon, Huntingdon, Kent, Leicester, Norfolk, Pembroke, Richmond, Salisbury and Winchester. In some cases the problem was a lack of male heirs: when the last of William the Marshal's five sons died in 1245, not a single one had fathered a son, and the lands of the earldom were divided between co-heiresses. In other cases, civil war or political action saw the extinction of an earldom. Simon de Montfort's earldom of Leicester was forfeited by his family on Simon's death at Evesham, and in the succeeding struggles the earl of Derby was compelled to give up his title and most of his lands.

The many changes in the earldoms could perhaps have provided immense opportunities for the crown to exercise patronage rights, and elevate new men to the status of earl, but in practice the number of new creations was small. Outside the royal family, creations were normally limited to men who had connections with the previous holders of a title. Simon de Montfort, for example, was made earl of Leicester in 1231. He was the youngest son of the previous earl, but his elder brother had handed over his claim to Simon. Under Edward i, the earldom of Arundel was granted to a distant relation of a previous earl in 1291, after a vacancy which had lasted since 1243. In 1306, the earldom of Richmond was entrusted to John of Brittany, in place of the hereditary claimant, John's elder brother. It was a startling innovation when, at the start of his reign, Edward ii created his Gascon favourite, Piers Gaveston, earl of Cornwall. The title had fallen into the crown's hands on the death of Earl Edmund in 1300, but the new holder had no family or other connection with the earldom.[2]

One reason why extinctions exceeded creations was that it was necessary to possess a substantial landed estate in order to be an earl. The fact that a title became vacant did not mean that there was necessarily someone available to take it up. Where an estate was divided between co-heiresses, it was very likely that none of their husbands would be of sufficient standing to receive the title. In the case of Hubert de Burgh, earl of Kent, who died in 1243, the title was entailed on the children of his third marriage. As there were none, the earldom fell vacant, and it was hardly appropriate to create it anew given Hubert's disgrace. The law provided few effective limitations to the king's freedom to do as he willed with the earldoms. When John the Scot, earl of Chester, died in 1237, he had as heirs two nieces, daughters of one of his sisters, and three other sisters. William de Forz, husband of the senior niece, claimed that the earldom was indivisible and that it should come to him in its entirety. It needed a full assembly of magnates before the matter was decided, in favour of dividing the earldom and its estates equally between all five claimants. That was a decision on a matter of law. Henry iii got round it by successfully buying out the various claimants. He compelled William de Forz to abandon all right to the title. Henry did this in his anxiety to acquire lands and position for his eldest son.

The crown did not strive to preserve earldoms. William Longsword, earl of Salisbury through marriage, an illegitimate son of Henry ii, was unable to hand on his comital title to his son William, though the latter tried in the courts to establish his right. In this case, the earldom of Salisbury was merged into that of Lincoln. In the aftermath of the Barons' Wars, the Ferrers family never accepted their loss of the title and status which the earldom of Derby had given them, but it could not be recovered through the courts. Under Edward i the earldom of Devon was extinguished when Isabella de Forz died: her rightful heir, Hugh de Courtenay, was deprived of his right by legal chicanery on the part of the crown. When Roger Bigod, earl of Norfolk, died childless in 1306, arrangements had been made which meant that no collateral should inherit the earldom. It duly came into the hands of the crown.

It would be wrong to try to read deep motives on the part of the crown in all this: the intention was not to weaken the English nobility so as to enhance the power of the monarchy, but much more simply to provide adequately for the royal family. Younger brothers and sons of the king needed earldoms and needed wealth, and the best way to achieve that end was to manipulate the upper end of the land market. Henry iii's brother Richard was made earl of Cornwall in 1227. The king's eldest son Edward was granted the earldom of Chester in 1254, and his second son Edmund was given Simon de Montfort's earldom of Leicester in 1265. He then became earl of Lancaster in 1267. This policy eventually resulted in a concentration of earldoms in the hands of Thomas of Lancaster, Edward ii's cousin. After the death of his father-in-law, the earl of Lincoln, in 1311, he held no less than five earldoms in his own hands, those of Lancaster, Lincoln, Leicester, Salisbury and Derby.

The king had to provide for his daughters as well as his sons. Initially Edward i favoured marriages with foreign princes, but in his later years he looked to English earls as husbands. Joan of Acre married the earl of Gloucester in 1290, and Elizabeth later married the earl of Hereford. Henry III needed to find fitting matches for his foreign relations, and so his Lusignan nieces from Poitou were found suitable husbands in the form of the heirs to the earldoms of Gloucester and Derby. These family links between the earls and the king did not, of course, always mean that close political links were established. Simon de Montfort, Henry III's most formidable opponent, was also his brother-in-law. Gilbert de Clare was not neutralised in political terms either by his first marriage to Alice de Lusignan, or by his second to Joan of Acre, Edward I's daughter. Thomas of Lancaster was both Edward II's cousin and his bitter enemy. Yet the family policy was one which brought the earldoms into a closer relationship with the crown and increased the king's influence over them.

Wide acres were the fundamental basis of the wealth and power of the magnates, but the character of their power changed during the thirteenth century. The traditional relationship between lords and their tenants was weakening, and new contractual links were forged as lordship in the old sense was being replaced by patronage.

In order to exercise power, a magnate needed a substantial following. In John's reign, the feudal bond, whereby a man held his land from a lord in return for military and other services, was still surprisingly powerful. Lists drawn up at the end of the civil war, in 1217, show that men were strongly inclined to follow their lords. Of the thirty-three tenants of William de Mowbray whose politics can be identified, thirty were certainly rebels. On the royalist side, the earl of Chester's Cheshire vassals followed him almost to a man, and only one rebel was to be found among the tenants of the amazonian Nicolaa de la Haye, the heroine of the defence of Lincoln. There were some exceptions: where a lord had only relatively recently acquired an estate, he might not have had time to win the loyalty of the tenants. Thus the tenants of the honour of Richmond were almost all rebels, for it was only in 1205 that the honour had been granted to the loyalist Ranulf, earl of Chester. It is striking that without baronial leadership, the tenants as a body showed a considerable degree of political solidarity. Where lordships had escheated to the crown, sympathies were, not surprisingly, likely to lie with the rebel cause. In those cases, and there were many, where men held land from more than one lord, a greater degree of independence was to be expected from the tenant.[3]

By the middle of the thirteenth century feudal bonds had become weaker, as is well demonstrated by one case, that of David de Esseby, a tenant of Henry de Hastings, an ardent Montfortian. Henry initially forced his tenant to follow his own political line by threatening him with distraint on his lands and goods, but this was only partially effective. David wisely appealed to the earl of Gloucester, paying his steward ten marks in order to have the earl's protection.[4] The deaths of many earls in this period had an adverse effect on the force of feudal bonds: a man such as William Mauduit, who received the earldom of Warwick in 1263, would not at once have the loyalty from the tenants that his predecessor had received.

If tenants could not be relied upon to support their lord, where could the latter turn? It was possible to retain men by contracting for their services, offering annual fees, wages, and gifts of robes. Analysis of the entourage of one mid-thirteenth-century magnate, Roger de Quincy, earl of Winchester, is suggestive. He was a rather exceptional figure in possessing substantial Scottish estates in addition to those he held in England: he was, indeed, constable of Scotland. Examination of the witness lists of his charters yields the names of 315 people associated with him. There were some fifteen knights who can be regarded as part of the earl's inner circle, and thirteen more who appeared with less regularity. Some of the knights were related to Earl Roger. Two men served him in the office of steward. They were not tenants of his, but came from the group of professional administrators. Only two of the earl's knightly tenants appeared with any regularity as witnessing his charters. Then there were a number of apparently landless knights, at least two of whom were in receipt of annual fees of 100 s. arranged by the earl. The knights of the outer circle fit into similar categories. There were thus different types of knights in Earl Roger's service. Some served for many years, perhaps even for life, while others obviously moved from one noble household to another. There were in addition, chaplains and clerks and, more surprisingly, some burgesses, but they witnessed only charters relating to the earl's borough of Brackley, and should not be regarded as regular members of his entourage.[5]

A list survives from 1297 for the household of the earl of Norfolk, Roger Bigod. This suggests a similar pattern to Roger de Quincy's following. It shows that Bigod could rely on the service of five bannerets, nine knights, some seventeen squires, and seven clerks.[6] In contrast to the evidence available for Roger de Quincy, this list provides a snapshot of the core of Bigod's following at one particular time. In the case of one of the bannerets, John de Segrave, the contract made by him with the earl has survived. It reveals that he was obliged to serve with fifteen knights, and their servants, receiving in turn robes for himself and his men, and was granted the manor of Lodden with the advowson of the church there. In war, Segrave would receive wages from the earl. If each of Bigod's bannerets served on similar terms, he would have been provided with a force of eighty cavalrymen, or over a hundred if the knights and squires on the list are included as well. This tallies with a contract the earl made with the government in the winter of 1297, to serve against the Scots with 130 cavalry. Resources in men on that scale suggest the political strength of the magnates. At the same time there was relatively little continuity in these magnate retinues. An earlier list of Bigod's dates from 1294–5, and shares only five names with the 1297 list. Similarly, examination of Aymer de Valence's following in Edward I's Scottish wars show only two men, Roger Inkpen and his son, campaigning regularly with him. No names appear more than once in Henry Percy's retinue.[7] This was not a stable system. The political implications are evident: it was possible for magnates to buy support on a large scale, but there was no consistency in that support, no solidity in the ties linking men to lords.

The reasons for the transformation of feudal bond into contractual bond were complex. It was inevitable as generation succeeded generation that the personal links between lord and feudal tenant would, in many cases, be reduced to little more than legal formality. The legal reforms of Henry II's day meant that tenants were given more protection against their lords. The tenants felt, no doubt, that they owed their lords less, the more secure their tenure became. Further legal developments in the Provisions of Westminster of 1259, and in the statutes of Edward I's reign, gave added strength to the position of tenants: it became more difficult to force them by means of distraint to perform services. Developments in military organisation, to be explained in a later chapter, meant that the whole body of tenants was no longer expected to turn out when a feudal summons was issued.

For the lords, the economic changes of the late twelfth and early thirteenth centuries, marked by a considerable price inflation, meant that it became more important than ever to maintain effective control over estates. Fixed rents and dues declined steadily in value. As a result it no longer made sense to grant land out as hereditary fiefs. It proved far better simply to retain men for life, or for a term of years, by assigning them rents or paying them a pension. The growing complexity of the business of running a great estate, with lands directly managed rather than granted out to subtenants, caused lords to recruit as stewards and bailiffs professional estate managers. It is perhaps something of an anachronism to use such a term: a baronial steward might well be an important knight in his own right. Simon of Kyme, a most important Lincolnshire man, served as Gilbert de Gant's steward in 1202: he had earlier been sheriff of Lincolnshire, and held lands in his own right from at least twelve different baronies.[8]

The precise terms on which such a man was retained in the early thirteenth century are not known, but it is clear that magnates did not rely solely on their own tenants when particular expertise was required. Stewards at this period, as later, would not serve one master for their whole career, but would move from one lord to another, and sometimes also serve the crown. Magnates also needed to hire lawyers to represent them in the king's courts. All this was best done by granting men fees and robes, retaining them rather than turning them into feudal tenants.

This practice of retaining is often known as 'bastard feudalism', and is more frequently associated with the fourteenth and fifteenth centuries than with the thirteenth. The earliest actual surviving indentures of retainer detailing the contractual arrangements date only from 1270. It would be wrong to make too much of this, for there is sufficient evidence already found, and no doubt more to be unearthed, to show that the system was prevalent at a much earlier date. In 1203 a letter patent was produced in court, to testify that William de Weston had been retained by William de Hommet to be a member of his household for an expedition to Jerusalem. A lawsuit in 1220 in which Henry de Bucuinte brought a case to obtain arrears of a pension of four marks a year granted him during John's reign by Gilbert de Heyndon is one example of a lord retaining someone in his service by means of a cash annuity instead of an enfeoffment with land. In another case, dating from 1250, Robert de Mapledurham sued Gerard de Oddingseles for arrears of his pension. Gerard claimed in reply that Robert had not performed the expected services. In the late 1250s William de Percy granted £5 p.a. to Ivo de Joneby in return for household service. It was laid down that Ivo was not to leave William's *mesnie* without permission. An inquisition taken after the royalist victory at Evesham revealed that John Fortin had received robes from the younger Simon de Montfort.[9] Such examples amply demonstrate the importance of retaining as a social bond prior to the first survivals of actual indentures.

The formal links of the feudal structure, and the force of the bonds of retainer, go only a small way to explaining the way in which magnates obtained support. It was necessary for lords to provide for the interests of their followers: if they did not do so, they would soon lose their backing. The revolt of Richard the Marshal in 1233 was precipitated by Henry III's cancellation of a grant to Gilbert Basset of the manor of Upavon in Wiltshire. Gilbert was a member of the circle connected to the Marshal, who duly felt obliged to assist him.[10]

In a wider sense, the need great men had to provide good lordship towards their supporters helps to explain why there is so much emphasis in so many of the major reforming enactments of the period on the interests not of the magnates themselves, but of their tenants and knights. Altruism should not be discounted as a motive: there is no reason to doubt that much was done because it was thought to be right. At the same time, if magnates were to obtain support, it made sense for them to advocate the kind of remedies that would appeal to their followers. The Protest of the Bachelors in 1259, when a group probably formed from knights and retainers complained about the failure of the reformers to put their fine intentions into practice, is the best indication of the kind of pressure from below that the magnates might experience.

No matter how powerful his retinue, no magnate could act effectively without the support of other great men. Family relationships were very significant in achieving this. There were complex links through marriage between some of King John's leading opponents: Robert de Ros and Eustace de Vesci were brothers-in-law, and Eustace's mother was Nicholas de Stuteville's sister. William de Forz, count of Aumale, was married to a daughter of Richard de Muntfichet: both men were among the twenty-five barons of Magna Carta.[11] There were also marriage connections between the lords of the Welsh marches who played such an important role in determining the outcome of the Barons' War of 1264–5.

The force of these family links is not always easy to assess. Families might be divided as well as united by political attitudes. The younger Marshal sided with the rebels against

John, whereas his father supported the king. Humphrey de Bohun, son of the earl of Hereford, and Roger Mortimer fought on opposite sides at Evesham, even though they were married to sisters. The best example is that of Simon de Montfort himself, married to the king's sister, a match which led to arguments rather than friendship with Henry III.

The chroniclers of John's reign identified the king's opponents in simple regional terms, as 'Northerners'. This was not wholly accurate, but provided a convenient shorthand. The role of the marcher lords in the Barons' wars of the mid-thirteenth century suggests not the solidarity of a county community, but the common ties of men who met frequently, who faced common problems, and who no doubt hunted and amused themselves together. The significance of regional bonds is also shown by the fact that of the 130 or so identifiable supporters of Simon de Montfort, over a hundred were landowners in the midland shires. They were not simply following a lead set by their feudal superiors: many must have been influenced by friends and neighbours.[12] A regional analysis is harder to apply to the resistance to Edward I in 1297, or to that to his son up to 1311, simply because those movements attracted such extensive support. Yet it may be significant that it was near Montgomery in the Welsh March that Edward I's opponents began to build up their strength in 1297. The Marcher lords felt that their liberties and rights were under particular threat, and provided a core to the movement.

A shared political purpose was not always sufficient to bind men together. An ill-defined but sometimes deeply felt sense of community, of joining together in a common enterprise, might not be enough, as the desertions from the baronial cause under Simon de Montfort's leadership showed. Those who opposed King John did not, it seems, feel the need to reinforce the ties forged by their hatred of the king with any formal documents. The violently fluctuating political world of the late 1250s and 1260s was a different matter. It was necessary to reinforce the links of common interest and concern with oaths and formal documents. At the very start of the crisis, on 12 April 1258, a group of magnates swore to assist each other to do right against all people. There was no specific pledge to promote reform, but that was the strong implication of the oath. The king's son Edward made two formal agreements in 1259, one with the earl of Gloucester in March, and one the following October, in which he swore to assist Simon de Montfort and his allies. The first of these reminded Powicke 'that we are dealing with a feudal society', but there is nothing feudal about the document, which in fact suggests a society that was seeking new ways of securing political bonds.[13] Documents of this sort have survived very much by chance, and it seems likely that there were many other such bonds made, and almost certainly broken. There was a definite group of men, mostly young, associated with Edward. Some were Marchers, such as Roger Clifford and Hamo Lestrange; another, Roger Leyburn from Kent, was Edward's steward. It seems probable that written agreements helped to cement the bonds of common interest and political ideals in their case. There was, however, no effective way of guaranteeing that such agreements could be kept: Edward was notorious in these years for his unreliability. Clauses appointing arbitrators in cases of disagreement were as unlikely to be effective as were the ecclesiastical sanctions applied to oaths.

The great crisis of Edward I's reign, that of 1297, threw up no written agreements between the earls, but Roger Bigod, earl of Norfolk, made an indenture with John de Segrave which shows the earl making efforts to build up a powerful following. At the start of Edward II's reign a group of the old king's councillors made a mutual pact, which was guaranteed by threats of excommunication, by one of their number, the bishop of Durham. The purpose of this political pact was expressed in regrettably ambiguous terms. The rights of the crown were to be maintained, but 'the oppressions which have taken place and are still taking place daily against the people should be redressed and amended'.[14]

This was not a political manifesto intended for publication, and no doubt those who made the agreement knew full well what it meant, but there was safety in imprecision. As

40

Edward II's reign proceeded, different forms of political compact were developed, in which the threats of excommunication of the 1308 agreement were replaced by possibly more effective threats of financial penalties.

Much of the political activity of the nobles took place in the king's councils and parliaments. Military musters provided further opportunities for discussion. There must have been many other occasions when great men met and debated their grievances, but there was no organised forum. Tournaments provided one opportunity. In 1297 the barons organised their own assembly near Montgomery, but such meetings were not common. Tournaments were one way of bringing great men together. They are often thought of as being little more than a useful training for battle, and indeed at this period they often were almost indistinguishable from war. This was not the age of the joust, of single combat between champions riding in the lists. Rather, tournaments were small-scale battles, organised in advance, in which the two sides would attack *en masse*. There would be few, if any, common soldiers involved, and there was a measure of organisation. As well as being military occasions, these could be political gatherings, or give rise to political animosity. In the 1250s there were tournaments between the aliens of Henry III's court, and English magnates, just as there were tournaments between Piers Gaveston and his men, and the English magnates early in Edward II's reign. Under John, in 1215, some of the barons held tournaments as a means of disguising the fact that they were recruiting armies. In 1228 the pope forbad tournaments in England because he claimed that they were the occasion for plots against the king. In 1260 Henry III forbad a tournament at Blythe, because he feared the political consequences of such a gathering. There was a steady stream of such prohibitions in the thirteenth century, testifying to the political dangers involved in such meetings rather than to the undoubted physical risk involved in participation in tournaments.[15]

The various agreements that magnates made with each other, the family alliances, the methods of building up retinues, did not provide the foundation stones of political parties in any real sense. They were attempts to provide the mortar needed to prevent the collapse of what were often very temporary alignments. It was all too easy for the crown, with all the weapons that it had at its disposal, to detach men from political groupings.

The crown had many ways in which it could try to control the nobility. Financial pressure could be brought to bear, though there were dangers that in doing this, a magnate's hostility to the crown might be reinforced. The imposition of heavy reliefs and fines by King John has often been cited as a major reason for baronial resentment. William FitzAlan was charged 10,000 marks (£6,666) to succeed to his barony. Nicholas de Stuteville promised the same sum to have his brother's lands. John de Lacy was asked to pay £7,000 to obtain the lands his father had held. Magnates were not in a position to pay such huge sums at once and John could use the threat of collecting them as a means of compelling good behaviour. After Magna Carta set limits on the rates at which reliefs could be imposed, the crown could no longer create indebtedness so easily. The old debts were not written off, however. In a well-known incident in 1295 Edward I was able to force the earl of Arundel and a group of other magnates to go to fight in Gascony against their wishes, simply by threatening to collect the debts that they owed to the crown. Most of Arundel's debts dated back to the relief imposed on William FitzAlan by John. Exchequer pressure on Roger Bigod, earl of Norfolk, in the early 1290s was a factor which helps to explain why he was one of the leaders of opposition in 1297, but after the crisis of that year Edward effectively neutralised the earl in political terms by playing on his indebtedness to the crown, which stood at about £1,800.[16]

Henry III took a very different view of magnate indebtedness from his father and from his son. His inclination was to try to maintain domestic peace by adopting a benevolent attitude towards the great men of the realm. Exchequer attempts to collect debts were frequently hindered by the king. Low instalments were set for repayment, and debts were often pardoned. Analysis of the baronial twelve of 1258 (or rather of the eleven laymen in the twelve) shows that the king was not using indebtedness to compel loyalty. Nor can financial pressure be adduced as a reason why men opposed the king.[17]

More subtle methods of winning allegiance included the careful use of patronage. Financial favours and grants of lands and rights might be given. Those magnates close to Henry III could expect to receive a flow of profitable wardships and escheats. There was also the common currency of small grants that men in favour would expect to receive. In 1251, for example, the earl of Gloucester was given five royal deer; two years later he received a life exemption from summonses before the king's justices in eyre. In the period of the Barons' Wars, the chroniclers were clear that those who abandoned the baronial cause did so as a result of bribery by the crown. The Tewkesbury annalist condemned those who in 1258 abandoned the cause of the Provisions of Oxford: they had been lured by promises of wide lands and powerful castles into abandoning their sworn allegiance.[18] Offers of lands were seen by some as the main means by which the future Edward I built up the party of marcher lords which assisted him to final victory at Evesham. When he came to the throne Edward was chary of using patronage on a wide scale, but when necessary, he was very ready to buy the backing he needed. In 1297 the earl of Warwick was, according to the Evesham chronicle, bribed by the king to abandon the opposition alliance. Very properly, substantial rewards went to Edward's military commanders after the Welsh war of 1282–3, and lands and honours were promised on a large scale in Scotland to those who fought for him there. The earl of Lincoln gained the honour of Denbigh in north Wales, and the lands of James the Steward in Scotland. Not surprisingly, his loyalty to Edward was unquestioning.

It is not always possible to provide straightforward answers to explain why magnates took one side or the other at times of crisis. There are many examples from John's reign of men changing their allegiance in the difficult days of 1215 and

1216. William de Forz, titular count of Aumale, was one of the twenty-five barons on the committee specified by Magna Carta, but within a couple of months he was supporting the king. John's grant to him of the manor of Driffield in Yorkshire may not be unconnected with this change. In 1216 he backed the French prince Louis for a time, then rejoined the royalist cause. He had, exceptionally, not been charged any relief, or inheritance duty, when he succeeded to his estates – a fact which led one historian to suggest that this favour was one of the rewards for 'distinguished service in the royal bed' on the part of his mother, Hawisia.[19] Financial inducements on the one hand, and friendship with such baronial partisans as Robert de Ros on the other, no doubt jostled one against the other in the mind of a confused young man.

The careers of the earls of Gloucester in the mid-century provide another example of apparently volatile political behaviour. Earl Richard had been a member of the court circle, but in 1258 he emerged as a leader of the reformers. He could not co-operate with Simon de Montfort, however, and by 1261 supported the restoration of Henry III's authority. He died in 1262 and his son initially supported Simon de Montfort, perhaps as a means of obtaining his inheritance before he reached his full majority. There followed a brief alliance with the king, but at Lewes the young earl fought with Montfort. He soon became dissatisfied with Montfort's autocratic rule. The scale of favours to Montfort's sons was one grievance, and Montfort's failure to eject all foreigners from the kingdom was another. Accordingly, he made common cause with Prince Edward, and fought on the winning side at Evesham. Political calculation no doubt played its part in the various changes of sides by the earls of Gloucester, while the story also suggests the importance of personal likes and dislikes within the small aristocratic élite.[20]

It is not possible to draw an identikit picture of a typical thirteenth-century baron. The nobility were a group of very different individuals, who responded in varied ways to the challenges that faced them. The one detailed life of a noble of this period that survives is that of William the Marshal, the hero of Henry iii's minority. This splendid work was written by the Marshal's squire, John of Erley, to demonstrate that William was the embodiment of all the chivalric knightly virtues: it is hard to crack the veneer. For one historian, the life shows that the Marshal 'was blessed with a brain too small to impede the natural vigour of a big, powerful and tireless physique'. In reality, the work proves the force of a very different verdict on the English nobles: 'Tough and greedy prize-fighters half their time, they had need of other qualities than their virility and a thick skull'.[21] William can be depicted, on the one hand, as an elderly quixotic fool, who would have rushed headlong into battle without donning his helmet, had his squire not pointed out that he had forgotten this most vital piece of equipment. On the other, he was the statesman who guided the country through the difficult initial years of Henry iii's minority. Thorough examination of his military career reveals a careful man, well versed in the trickery of war as well as in the principles of chivalry. He had no compunction about using the terror methods of the cavalry raid, or chevauchée, and the wisdom to avoid set-piece battles in open country. A man who rose from being a landless younger son to become the most respected noble in the land, a man who survived all the political vicissitudes of the reigns of Henry ii, Richard, John, and the first years of Henry iii, can hardly be categorised as unintelligent. The Marshal knew how best to manipulate and take advantage of the cultural values of the day. Loyalty and honour were skilfully deployed not in pursuit of a romantic, unattainable ideal, but in the practical acquisition of lands and power.[22]

Few nobles could match the prestige of the Marshal. Some were clearly disreputable: Robert Ferrers, earl of Derby in the 1260s, seems to have been a young man of little sense, much given to violence, who lost his earldom as result of his folly in antagonising the heir to the throne and his brother. In contrast, Henry de Lacy, earl of Lincoln, and contemporary of Edward i, was a man of great repute, a most loyal servant of the crown until he was driven to oppose the follies of Edward II. Some were good businessmen: Edmund, earl of Cornwall, cousin of Edward I, accumulated vast wealth. Roger Bigod, earl of Norfolk in the later thirteenth century, in contrast, seems to have been a spendthrift who could not manage his financial affairs. He borrowed from his brother, was heavily in debt to the crown, and lost political influence as a result of his problems. Neither Edmund nor Roger made a success of their personal life: Edmund's wife separated from him and went into a nunnery, while Roger failed to father any heirs.

It would be unfair to saddle so varied a group of men with simple generalisations about their attitudes and abilities. They faced, no doubt, similar problems in maintaining their rights, in looking after their lands and inheritances, and adopted broadly similar solutions to the questions of how to build up a retinue and how to organise estates. As individuals they differed greatly, and their responses to the political problems of the age varied widely. It used to be the fashion to denigrate the nobility: it is now the fashion to praise them. Some thirteenth-century English nobles deserve the first treatment, and others the second. A sympathetic understanding of these men is needed if the politics of the period is to become comprehensible.

3
THE COUNTY COMMUNITY

THE MAGNATES were the leaders of political society, but they did not, and could not, act alone. The knights and others, who formed what may anachronistically be termed the gentry, had their grievances, and played their part in public affairs. The complexity of royal administration in the shires meant that knights were increasingly drawn into public affairs, sitting on juries, assessing and collecting taxes, recruiting troops, maintaining public order and undertaking multifarious other tasks essential to the good running of the country. The interface between royal government and local gentry society was often jagged. Grievances accumulated, adding to the tensions of political affairs. Recent work has stressed the way in which these grievances were articulated in the county communities. The horizontal links which brought men together in such communities have been stressed in contrast to the vertical links provided by lordship. A further debate has taken place as to whether the gentry's role in politics was founded on a self-confidence drawn from economic success, or whether they were driven to act by economic misfortune.

There is no doubting the importance of knightly grievances in this period. This was already clear in John's reign. Magna Carta did not confine itself to the problems faced by the baronage. Various clauses of the Charter provided assistance to the knights and tenants of great lords against arbitrary action. The latter, for example, could only levy aids to pay for their own ransoms, the knighting of their eldest sons, and the marriage of their eldest daughters, similar limitations to those placed on the king himself. The promise that in future only men with a good knowledge of the law should be appointed as justices, constables, sheriffs or bailiffs provides a commentary on the inadequate character of local administration. Some protection was provided for heirs whose inheritance was severely encumbered by debts owed to Jewish moneylenders, a significant problem for growing numbers of knights and others. The various clauses which provided guarantees for 'free men' in the Charter, such as clause 20 limiting fines, or the celebrated clause 39 promising judgement by peers and the law of the land, have been the subject of much argument. A 'free man' was exactly what it said, but in practice, it was perhaps 'free men' of the knightly class who might expect to benefit most from such measures.

The significance of knightly and tenant grievances was also very evident in the years 1258–65. The barons made it clear that in their dealings with their own tenants they should observe the same good laws and customs that they expected the king to apply to them. The Provisions of Westminster of 1259 contained much that was in the interests of the tenants. The question of whether baronial administration should be subject to the same degree of investigation as were royal officials was none the less contentious. Simon de Montfort and the more radical reformers were definite that the running of private franchises needed examining: the earl of Gloucester was of a different opinion. Inquisitions held after Simon's defeat at Evesham reveal very clearly the considerable depth of knightly support, particularly in the Midlands, that he received.

The future Edward I, for a brief period, supported his uncle Simon de Montfort against the king, and when he came to the throne he displayed an awareness of the importance of the positive side of the reform movement. Much of the thrust of the Provisions of Westminster, as applied to government and law in the localities, was given a new impetus in the first Statute of Westminster of 1275. In 1278 new appointments gave the counties the kind of local men as sheriffs that they had demanded in 1258. The efficacy of Edward's measures helps to explain why there was not more evidence of discontent in the shires, particularly in the first half of his reign.

In Edward's later years problems increased. There was much resentment from the class of £20 landholders at his plans to compel them to serve in Flanders in 1297. In 1300 the king conceded the right of local election of sheriffs to the counties in a move echoing arguments that had surfaced on several occasions during the thirteenth century. Disputes over the boundaries of the royal forest at the end of Edward's reign also revived arguments that had much concerned the knights and gentry intermittently for many years. The graph of knightly involvement in politics did not climb steadily: the Ordinances of 1311 were a baronial document, providing for baronial consent in parliament in many areas of royal policy. There is no direct evidence of knightly involvement. Even so, many of the problems tackled in the Ordinances were matters of great concern to the knights and baronial tenants.

Was it through the county communities that the knights and gentry found their political voice? Historians of the seventeenth century have made much of the importance of the county community in their period, and medievalists have sought to impose similar patterns on earlier ages. Susan Reynolds has stressed the significance of collective structures in society, as against the hierarchical ties of kingship and lordship that have usually been emphasised. More specifically, J. R. Maddicott has pointed to the importance of county communities in the political struggles of the first half of the thirteenth century. Few historical arguments are wholly new: in the nineteenth century Stubbs laid stress on the county community, suggesting that the crown may have seen in the knights of the shire a potential counterweight to the power of the baronage. Yet study by a legal historian, R. C. Palmer, of the central institution of the shire, the county court, yields an interpretation which it is hard to equate with the notion of the growing political importance and independence of the knights and gentry.[1]

The county, or shire, was a well-established institution in England. Originating in Wessex, the shire system was introduced into the Midlands and further north during the expansion of Wessex in the tenth century. In the far north, however, the system came later, being developed in the Norman period. Although it may look fairly uniform, there were very considerable variations in this structure. Kent and Sussex were shires, but they possessed many peculiarities which went back to the days when they were independent kingdoms: for example, Sussex was subdivided into rapes, rather than the normal hundreds. Such shires which dated back into the dim mists of Anglo-Saxon obscurity may have had a greater sense of unity and tradition than others of more recent origin, though the point is unprovable. The counties of the old Danelaw region were distinctive in many ways. The great shires of Yorkshire and Lincolnshire were each divided into three ridings or parts. Within them were wapentakes, not hundreds, though this distinction was a purely verbal one. The division of East Anglia into Norfolk and Suffolk was relatively late: these two counties, like Derbyshire and Warwickshire, and Huntingdonshire and Cambridgeshire, normally shared a single sheriff. Some county boundaries were very odd: there were small enclaves of Worcestershire which lay within Gloucestershire and Warwickshire. Rutland was a tiny anomaly which had its origins in the Norman period. Within a county there might be liberties, particularly ecclesiastical ones, which were largely independent of the workings of the shire administration. The Isle of Ely, controlled by the abbot, was virtually an independent county within Cambridgeshire. Bury St Edmunds possessed a major liberty in Suffolk, and there are many other examples. Yet, although the counties were so diverse, administrative convenience dictated that the government should treat all in the same way. When orders were sent out to all sheriffs, the writs were all identically worded.

The chief royal official in charge of the county was the sheriff. He was appointed in the exchequer, and was answerable to the exchequer for the revenues of the county. The terms of appointment varied at different times in the course of the thirteenth century, and so did the character of the men nominated. Under John, many counties were put into the hands of trusted courtier barons such as Hugh de Neville and Hubert de Burgh. By the end of the century, no such men were ever appointed as sheriffs, and the office had clearly declined in political importance. Changes in the financial policy of the exchequer do much to explain this. As more stringent terms were imposed on the sheriffs, heaping increments on the existing farms, or annual sums that they owed, so the office became less and less popular among great men. The major political changes of 1236, which followed the establishment of William of Savoy as the king's chief councillor, saw curial sheriffs depart from office. Changes took place in seventeen counties. None of the new men were courtiers, but many had played a considerable part in local administration in the past. It was presumably the exchequer officials who selected men of what might be termed gentry status, who were of known competence. Some *curiales* were appointed later, but the situation did not favour them. A great man would expect to appoint a deputy to do the work on the spot, and he would hope to be able to make a handsome profit out of office. With the exchequer tightening the screws, there was little to be gained for a great man in obtaining a sheriffdom, and men of lesser standing were employed instead. They were not given so much authority as their curial predecessors: one corollary of the change in the standing of the sheriff was that many castles were entrusted to special constables, rather than left in the charge of the sheriff. It was an article of faith in the shires that sheriffs should be local men, landholders in the county where they held office, accountable to local society as well as to the crown, a demand made emphatically in the 1258 Provisions of Oxford. The fact that many sheriffs under Henry III were not local men was a matter of considerable grievance in the localities.[2]

The shire court provided the county community with its institutional focus. Unfortunately, few records from county courts survive, and the county which is best documented, Cheshire, is regrettably abnormal in various ways, for it had a remarkable degree of freedom from royal jurisdiction, and by the late thirteenth century possessed a similar palatine status to Durham. Counties varied in the pattern of court meetings. In some there was one single place of meeting, in others there were several. This was important: in the case of Kent, where the court met in a large number of different places, it seems unlikely that all the influential men of the shire would in fact all meet on every occasion. To have many meeting places surely deprived a county of unity. Meetings were usually held every four weeks, although six weeks was also known. These courts traditionally met for no more than one day, and there was resistance when sheriffs attempted to extend the sessions. In 1284 a Devon knight, Thomas le Pruz, prevented the sheriff from holding the session after the meal on the second day: there continued to be resistance to lengthening the sessions unduly. Meetings might take place in the open air, as at Pennenden Heath in Kent, in a castle or even a house. The Oxfordshire court generally met in the king's manor hall in the city. That of Huntingdonshire met in the aisles of the chapel of Huntingdon castle. By the late thirteenth century it was becoming more common for a special building to be put up for the meetings to take place. The choice of such meeting places does not suggest that the assemblies were large ones.

In theory, when the county court was summoned before royal justices, the sheriff was supposed to request the attendance of all archbishops, bishops, abbots, priors, earls, barons, knights and all free tenants, as well as four men and the reeve from each vill, and twelve burgesses from each town. But this was no more than theory. The reality was substantially different. It was obviously necessary for the judges to attend: they were probably drawn from the ranks of those with both experience and prestige in the shire. Then there were the suitors of the court. Many landholders were obliged by the terms of their tenure to perform suit of court, either in person or by sending a substitute. Numbers of suitors varied. In the 1230s the number of Cambridgeshire suitors totalled about 160, but it fell as the century proceeded to roughly 100. Shropshire had 102 suitors in 1255; Oxfordshire in 1279 over sixty, but no more than eight suitors were obliged to attend each session of the court. Until Edward I's reign the obligation seems to have been regarded seriously. Sheriffs fined men for not appearing when they should have done, and men found it worth while to obtain royal grants exempting them from suit of court. Under Edward the system was in decline, and R. C. Palmer has concluded that 'Suitors, by and large, played little or no role in the normal county procedure by around 1300, even though their liability and their role according to legal theory remained unchanged'. It was even claimed in 1303 that in Warwickshire and Leicestershire there were no suitors of the county courts. Palmer argues that 'the actual functioning of the county court was dominated by the barons of the county through their legal experts, the stewards and bailiffs'. He points to evidence from as early as 1114, from Burton Abbey, showing that Edric the Old, a reeve, went to pleas, both in the county and the hundred, for the abbot's land. In 1226 John Marshal's steward went to the court of Kesteven, one of the parts of Lincolnshire, on behalf of his lord, and there is further evidence for the practice of lords sending stewards to act on their behalf in the county courts. These men, expert in administration and law, held the key to the county courts: 'It was clearly the seneschals and bailiffs who dominated the county courts, at least when the bishops, abbots, earls and barons were not present'.[3]

The author of Bracton in a celebrated passage referred to the way in which justices might summon before them four or six of the important men in the county, known as *buzones*, who would be given detailed instructions about such matters as the organisation of the hue and cry. The word *buzones* is perhaps best translated as 'big shots' (*buzo* means crossbow bolt in Latin), but this does not help much in identifying these influential figures. In 1922 G. T. Lapsley discussed a Gloucestershire case of 1212, in which the *buzones*, exceptionally, were named, and he proceeded to analyse the careers of these men. The task was not an easy one, as evidence is scarce. One example is perhaps enough. One of the *buzones* was Walter de Aure, 'a relatively dim figure' as Lapsley calls him. Awre, says Lapsley, was acquired by Walter by 1204 at the latest, but his family had an earlier connection with the place. He also had a profitable interest in some salt pans near Gloucester, and was involved in the Forest of Dean iron trade. He had been given the right of not being impleaded for any free tenement save before the king or chief justice. In 1207 he had been a tax assessor in Oxfordshire. He died in 1211. Lapsley concludes from this that he was 'a person of condition and some property in the county of Gloucester'. Palmer, in contrast, points out that Walter held Awre merely at farm, paying an annual sum to the king for it. He was not lord of the manor there, but held only two virgates and six acres. In various deeds around 1200 he was stated to be the bailiff of the hundred of Newnham, close to Awre. The tax commission related to Gloucestershire, not Oxfordshire, and Palmer concludes that Walter was 'a bailiff and lawyer, rather than a business-loving squire'. Whether such a clear distinction can be made between professional stewards and lawyers, and country gentlemen with a talent for business, may well be doubted: many stewards were members of notable county families, just as some were rising men of obscure origins.[4] As the thirteenth century progressed, however, the case for regarding the county court as being dominated by the professional administrators employed by the great men becomes ever stronger.

The institutional framework is, therefore, one in which the chief royal official in the county, the sheriff, was declining in status in the thirteenth century, and in which the increasingly ill-attended county courts were controlled by the estate managers of the great landlords. This hardly fits with the view of the period as one in which the county community was gaining in political importance, acquiring a new self-confidence and assertiveness.

How effective was the county community? A much-discussed incident took place in Lincolnshire in 1226, which shows it in action. The sheriff heard pleas in the county court from dawn to dusk, and then postponed the rest of the business until the next day. The knights of the county, however, refused to enter the court, arguing that the business should all be completed in the one day. The cases left over were then postponed to the wapentake courts, but in the Kesteven court the sheriff was prevented from giving judgement by two knights, Theobald Hautein and Hugh of Humby, who told him that he was acting contrary to Magna Carta, and that the business belonged rightly in the county court. The case shows an assertive local community appealing in defence of its privileges to Magna Carta. Yet there is some ambiguity. Much depends on how the leading figure in the protest, Theobald Hautein, is viewed. He was one of the many Lincolnshire knights who had joined the rebellion in 1215, and can be seen as a local knight defending local rights. Palmer, however, argues that he was no ordinary Lincolnshire knight, but a professional lawyer, who had acted 'infrequently but repeatedly' as an attorney in the king's court. Hautein had certainly been a steward, and it is very possible that he had magnate support for his protest. It is a remarkable feature that while the incident has been used by historians to show the strength of the local community in resisting a minion of central government, what the knights wanted was to limit the duration of the very meeting, the county court, that it is thought provided them with an institutional identity. Nor were Hautein and his colleagues correct in appealing to Magna Carta, for it did not actually provide them with what they wanted – it merely specified the proper interval between court sessions, not the length of the sessions themselves.[5]

In the early thirteenth century there was a strong desire to establish local rights and liberties at a county level. Counties paid money in return for particular favours and privileges.

Lancashire offered 100 marks in 1199 and again in 1204 to have Richard Vernon as sheriff. In 1210 the men of Somerset and Devon paid for the privilege of having a local man as sheriff, with the specific exclusion of William Briwerre. Many counties bought forest privileges. The practice continued in Henry III's early years: in 1221 or thereabouts Cornwall paid for the right of having a local man as sheriff, and in 1232 Nottinghamshire and Derbyshire paid to have Ralph Fitz-Nicholas as sheriff for life. He was a local landowner, who at the same time had influence at court, a factor which may have been seen as useful.[6]

These purchases of privileges were not followed up later by demands for further grants on the scale that might be expected, even though the government became increasingly reluctant to sell rights to county communities. The scale of resistance to Henry's government by the local communities appears limited. Arguments continued in Lincolnshire over the holding of the county court: in 1252 the king ordered the sessions to be held over two days when this was needed. In 1253 the knights of Shropshire objected to new peace-keeping arrangements which were modelled upon those of Savoy. The community of Chester protested at Henry's innovations in the way he administered it. Maddicott argues that in 1258 the demands previously expressed at the county level were articulated for the first time at a national level.[7] However, the scale of the individual requests by the county communities was negligible when compared to the collective demands of 1258. Instances where the crown summoned knights from the counties for such matters as the negotiation of taxes can hardly be taken as indications of the political force of the county assemblies, for the initiative came from above.

There can be no doubt at all that local grievances were highly important in the period of baronial reform and rebellion. The pressure that had been placed on local communities through the sheriffs, particularly since 1237, when the last general tax had been granted to the king, was immense. There were substantial grievances against royal, and, to some extent, baronial administration. Some magnates, particularly those linked to the court, had overridden local custom and defied local officials with impunity. These local grievances, however, did not surface at the outbreak of the crisis early in 1258. They emerged only as a result of inquiries set on foot by the reformers, with four knights to investigate each county. While first steps were taken to meet local grievances in the Provisions of the Barons in the autumn of 1258, it was not until the promulgation of the Provisions of Westminster a year later that they were properly tackled. This does not suggest that the county communities were articulate and organised in their demands for reform. Nor was it they, but rather the mysterious body terming itself 'the Community of the Bachelors of England', who protested at the slow pace of reform in the early autumn of 1259. As events lurched towards the final debacle of Evesham in 1265, there is surprisingly little evidence of the county communities as such taking a leading role. Simon de Montfort certainly received wide support from the knights and gentry of the Midlands, where his aristocratic leadership found no rivals.[8] It is not apparent, however, from the sources that this support was the result of any collective decisions taken by the county communities. It is far more likely to have been the result of the individual choice of those concerned.

Edward I's reign reveals few indications of independent action on the part of the county communities. In 1297 the county of Sussex, called upon to elect representatives for parliament, refused to do so because it was argued that the archbishop of Canterbury and other great men were not able to be present. The community was engaging in passive resistance to the king's demands in that year of crisis. In the same year the county community of Worcester challenged royal tax collectors, arguing that they would not agree to the collection of the tax until they had received the liberties that they were entitled to under the terms of Magna Carta and the Charter of the Forest. Most of the evidence of the actions of county communities concerns much less important matters. The county community of Cumberland complained that in their county there was no proper system of indictment of criminals, but that they could be arrested by bailiffs merely on suspicion, and the full operation of the common law in accordance with the statute of Winchester was requested. In contrast, at the end of the reign the county community of Shropshire protested against the application of the statute of Winchester, pointing out that its provisions were not compatible with local custom, and claiming that in the county there should be a general exemption from the burdens imposed on the hundreds by the statute.[9]

Under Edward, the practice of petitioning in parliament provided county communities with a new outlet for their grievances, but it can hardly be said that parliament was swamped with their complaints. The number of petitions from county communities was small, and the topics they raised were not notably important. The Cumberland community complained that when, in 1302, the sheriff had taken a certain number of cattle to provide for the royal larder, he had obtained due allowance in his accounts at the exchequer, but had not actually paid the money over in Cumberland. Only two county petitions survive from the 1270s: between 1290 and 1307, when documentation is fuller, there were twenty-three in all: less than one per parliament.[10] The main concern of the petitions was with the actions of royal officials and, in particular, malpractice on their part, rather than with broad political issues. A reading of the rolls of parliament does yield little indication that the county communities were important.

While the counties, in a formal institutional sense, did not provide a major focus for opposition to the crown, the other side of the picture is very different. Their value to the crown was immeasurable. The county courts were a vital channel of communication. It was there that proclamations were sent, and read out. In 1258 the famous announcement of Henry III's adherence to the reform scheme, the one state document in English of this period, was sent round to all the counties.

Copies of Edward I's statutes were publicised in the county courts. Negotiations might take place at a county level: in 1254 sheriffs were instructed to explain the king's financial need in the county courts, and to persuade those present to grant a tax, and select knights to report to the council on the deliberations. In 1301 the king chose to negotiate the levy of foodstuffs to supply the army at a county level, rather than risk putting the issue before a parliament. In every case the counties agreed to grant what the king's commissioners requested.

The ways in which the county was important to the crown were many and varied. In military organisation it is striking that, whereas the cavalry were formed into retinues, each led by a banneret or knight, with no regional affiliation indicated, the infantry were all listed in contingents set out county by county. The commissions of array which recruited the troops were appointed by counties: initially, one commission to several counties, later, each commission to one or two counties at most. Orders for the collection of food supplies were all sent to the sheriffs, and the task was organised on a county basis. Taxes were generally granted at the national level, but the collection was done county by county. The whole administrative structure relied on the county organisation, and this inevitably brought the men of administrative competence together within a county under the control of the sheriff. The county, in other words, was a royal creation, an administrative unit bound to the crown in many ways. This did not necessarily mean that it could not develop into a focus around which hostility to royal authority might be institutionalised, but it made this less likely.

If the counties in a formal sense were largely instruments of royal government, was it the case that local opinion was expressed in some more informal way at the county level? In studying the local society in fourteenth-century Sussex, Nigel Saul has suggested that it was in such activities as hunting that the gentry met together and exchanged views. Their social circles were not defined by county boundaries: the gentry of east Sussex had few connections with their peers in west Sussex.[11] The landholding structure of England was not formed in terms of county boundaries. This was obviously the case as far as great lordships were concerned: the earls of Gloucester held land right across southern England. At a lower level of society, even quite minor knights might well hold land in more than one shire. Nor were ecclesiastical boundaries the same as those of the counties. While there were obviously cultural differences of a regional character, it is impossible to identify the culture of an individual county. A cautious attempt to do so for Lincolnshire made use of one story as evidence because it contained a reference to Boston – yet it was written down at the priory of Worcester.[12] There were no county cricket teams with which men could identify in the thirteenth century, and evidence for the existence of a strong sense of loyalty to county is impossible to find in the sources.

In the period of the Barons' Wars it was to the commune, or community, of England that men felt loyalty, rather than to their county communities. FitzThedmar, the London chronicler, wrote that after Louis IX produced his arbitration at Amiens in favour of Henry III, the Londoners, the men of the Cinque Ports, and 'almost all the commune of the middling people of the realm of England' rejected it. In the much quoted Peatling Magna incident, a few days after Evesham, the men of Peatling Magna in Leicestershire attacked Peter de Nevill and his men as they were passing through, saying that they were going 'against the community of the realm and against the barons'.[13] There was no mention of the local county community here. In the inquiries held after the end of the civil war, when men's actions were explained, which was not often, it was in terms of their having been in the service of some magnate, and never of loyalty to the local community.

If local gentry society did not express its grievances through the county and the county community, how did it do so? The importance of lordship should not be ignored. Between 1207 and 1209 Peter de Brus granted his tenants in Cleveland a charter which, among other things, promised them that if any of them suffered forfeiture, 'it shall be assessed according to his chattels and according to the offence for which he incurred it'. This is very close to clause 20 of Magna Carta, which promised that fines would be related to the scale of the offence, and it is significant that Peter was one of the Northerners at the heart of opposition to King John.[14] In some circumstances the grievances of knights and tenants would have been known to their lords, and used politically by them. There was a danger in John's reign, and perhaps later, that if the magnates were not seen to be favouring the interests of their tenants, the king would offer the latter concessions to win their support. John's move in 1212 to relax debts owed to the Jews fits this pattern. A major problem prior to 1258 had been that Henry III had not conducted extensive investigations into local government. There was no effective mechanism for grievances to be brought forward, and the result was frustration and tension. Very important, therefore, as channels of communication were the great inquiries that were held in the second half of the thirteenth century. In 1258–9 the reforming council took great care to discover the grievances of local society, first, by sending the justiciar, Hugh Bigod, on a great eyre, and then by expanding this with a series of commissions to justices. Edward I was well aware of the importance of the reforms of the late 1250s and early 1260s for the localities, and he was a wise enough politician – or was sufficiently well advised – to see that further work was needed. He did not, however, seek the advice of the counties as they were represented in the county courts, but set up national inquiries. In 1274, for example, there was the great inquest which produced the Hundred Rolls, an astonishingly full investigation of government at the local level. In 1289 a general invitation was issued to his subjects to bring complaints against the judges and other royal officials. The initiatives were coming from above, not below. The practice of parliamentary representation remains to be discussed later, but here too, the indications are that the king was using the system to disseminate information to his subjects, not the reverse.

Was it the case that the political role, such as it was, of the knights and gentry sprang from their wealth and power in local society? Or were these groups attempting to maintain their position in the face of growing economic odds? As with the case of the county community, thirteenth century historians have attempted for their period to light the embers of a controversy which once raged among their seventeenth-century colleagues.[15] There are very considerable methodological problems involved. Counting knights – or knightly families – is not easy. By the late thirteenth century there were by one estimate no more than 1,250 actual knights in England. This almost certainly marks a considerable decline as against the twelfth century, but this was not necessarily the result of the economic decline of a class. Rather, it reflected the rapid increase in the costs of military equipment and a consequent change in the status of the knight. There is good evidence for monastic houses, such as Bury St Edmunds or Peterborough, buying up knightly property, and for the indebtedness of some knightly families to Jewish money-lenders, but while this reveals the difficulties some faced, it does not show that all knights faced similar problems. Examination of the knightly families of one county, Oxfordshire, does not suggest that dramatic changes were taking place in the course of the century, and demonstrates instead a striking continuity. Study of the career of the ambitious and unscrupulous Geoffrey de Langley, a forest official, shows him profiting from the decline of a number of knightly families. At the same time, Geoffrey's career shows the way in which a man could rise to power. The decline of some was balanced by the success of others.

It seems likely that some knightly families, such as the Chenduits of Oxfordshire, were incapable of taking advantage of the economic conditions of the period in the way that the holders of great estates could do. A sufficient number of individuals can be identified as finding times hard to suggest that economic difficulties contributed to political problems. Such men are far more likely to be found in the ranks of Simon de Montfort's supporters than among the royalists.

The knightly grievances which were met in the Provisions of Westminster were those of men facing problems in maintaining their status, not those of men thrusting their way to power. It would be very wrong, however, to interpret the problems facing knights in the thirteenth century in terms of a simple economic determinism. This was not a period of major economic crisis, and it was problems of government, not of estate management, which must be stressed.

The picture of the thirteenth century witnessing the rise of the knights to a new position of political importance, with demands initially articulated in county assemblies confident in their authority, and then collectively expressed in parliamentary politics, is an attractive one. Yet although the county communities can be seen as very active in the early thirteenth century, purchasing privileges from the crown, it is difficult to demonstrate that this was followed up effectively. Rather than making use of the county courts, the gentry of Lincolnshire wanted to limit sessions to no more than one day. The county was perhaps seen more as an instrument of royal government than as a bulwark against royal and baronial extortion. This is not to argue that knights and gentry played an unimportant role in the politics of the thirteenth century, or that their grievances were insignificant; merely that the county communities as such played a less important part than is sometimes claimed. The strength of gentry society lay in the informal connections that existed between families, in links through marriage, ties of lordship, traditional allegiances and mutual self-interest. Only to a very limited extent was this strength expressed through the formal organisation of the county, which with its courts and officials served the crown more than it did local society.

4

THE CHURCH

THE THIRTEENTH CENTURY has been viewed as an increasingly secular age, a period when the church no longer had the influence it had possessed in previous centuries. Yet the church cannot be ignored. It was closely involved in the world of politics. From Innocent III to Boniface VIII the papacy became more and more enmeshed in the power struggles of kings and nobles. There was not a straightforward clash between the ideologies of church and state in England: churchmen can be found both supporting the crown, and opposing it, as well as mediating in political disputes. The great prelates, archbishops, bishops and major abbots, were acknowledged to have an important place in the councils of the nation. It was only in 1297 that a parliament was held without any of the clergy being asked to attend. One distinctive contribution of the church was to inject into the great political disputes an intellectual element derived from the scholastic training provided by universities, which provided an additional fizz to what was already a heady brew. The papacy, too, had its part to play in English affairs during the period. Established powers generally support each other, and the crown benefited from the willingness of popes to annul unwelcome concessions, though this papal support could not always be relied upon.

Many bishops obtained their office after service in the royal administration. A good number were academics, university trained *magistri*. Some, such as Robert Grosseteste, the celebrated bishop of Lincoln under Henry III, were of obscure social origins; others, such as Walter Cantilupe of Worcester or his nephew Thomas Cantilupe of Hereford, came from well-established baronial families. There were also foreigners. Some, such as Boniface of Savoy, archbishop of Canterbury, or Aymer de Valence of Winchester, owed their position to their relationship to the royal family. John of Pontoise became bishop of Winchester in Edward I's reign as the result of being well placed at the papal Curia. Only a very few bishops rose from being monks: Edward I's first two archbishops of Canterbury, Kilwardby and Pecham, were both friars.[1]

The church was divided into two provinces, those of Canterbury and York: squabbles over whether the latter archbishop could travel through the southern province with his cross borne before him bedevilled relations between the two. Even within a province, there might be little unity. In the north, the relationship between York and Durham was not an easy one, and disputes such as that between John Pecham and Thomas Cantilupe demonstrate the problems that might occur between an archbishop and his suffragans. Political consistency could not emerge from such diversity.

John's reign well illustrates the ambivalent role of the church in political affairs. For some historians Archbishop Langton was the man who was responsible for turning a baronial rebellion into a wide-ranging reform programme; for others he was no more than an unsuccessful mediator between the king and his opponents. Initial hostility between John and Langton arose from the circumstances of the archbishop's appointment in 1207 at the hands of the pope, in place of John's nominee, John de Grey. An interdict was imposed on the kingdom, and excommunication of the king followed. Neither weapon was particularly effective, but by 1213 John very rightly saw that the pope might be a valuable ally. He performed fealty to a papal legate, and agreed to hold the kingdom as a fief from Rome. Langton returned to England: the interdict was removed, and the excommunication of the king lifted. Innocent lent his full support to John. Langton, however, did not follow his lead.

According to the chronicler Roger Wendover, it was Archbishop Langton who in an address at St Paul's in August 1213 read out Henry I's coronation charter, stressing that it showed how lost liberties could be regained. This evidence has been much criticised: there is a text of Langton's sermon at St Paul's, but it contains no mention of Henry I's charter. Study of the Petition of the Barons, and of Magna Carta itself, does not suggest that Langton or his fellow-bishops contributed much to the drafting of these documents, for there is very little that directly concerns the church. The first clause of Magna Carta guaranteed the rights and liberties of the church, but in only a very unspecific way. Clause 22 dealt with fines levied on the clergy, and the church's rights in cases of intestacy were guaranteed. Langton's role in the months preceding the issue of Magna Carta was ostensibly that of a mediator. Yet he certainly considered that the king's opponents had justified grievances, and in trying to achieve a settlement, his bias was a pro-baronial one.[2]

The papal contribution to the crisis was very different from that of the archbishop. Innocent III unintentionally played a part in originating what is probably the best-known clause of Magna Carta. On 19 March 1215 he wrote asking that the issue between the king and his barons should be settled by the judgement of peers in accordance with the law and custom of the land. John modified this in letters patent on 10 May, when he promised not to go against the barons save by the law of the realm or the judgement of peers in his court. The general principle was then set out in the celebrated clause 39 of Magna Carta, which stated that no free man should be taken or imprisoned, or have other action taken against him, except by lawful judgement of peers or by the law of the land.[3] In the short term, however, more important than this was Innocent's act annulling Magna Carta and his suspension of Langton from office in August and November 1215, actions which inflamed the situation rather than promoted peace. Magna Carta was, for Innocent, illegal and wicked, for it placed undue and improper limitations on the king's rights and dignity.

After John's death papal action was to provide the Charter with impressive status and authority. The reissues (with the more tendentious clauses removed) of the Charter in 1216 and 1217 took place under the auspices of the papal legate, Guala, who was acting alongside William the Marshal, the *rector* of the young king and the realm. As revised, the Charter did not limit royal power unduly, and it was not extracted from the king by coercion. The position of Guala and his successor as legate, Pandulf, was one of stalwart support for the regency government, while Langton did more in the 1220s to maintain the rights and position of the crown than he had done to weaken John's government a decade previously.[4]

Similar patterns can be observed later in the thirteenth century. Papal support for the crown was to be significant on several occasions. Magna Carta was not questioned: in its 1225 version it was confirmed by Innocent IV in 1245. Other concessions made by the crown, however, received rough handling. In 1260 Alexander IV condemned the Provisions of Oxford, and in 1264 the papal legate, Guy Foulquois, the future Clement IV, though unable to land in England, did all he could to work against Simon de Montfort, whom he excommunicated with his followers. Foulquois's successor as legate, Ottobuono, was even engaged in trying to raise forces on the continent for an invasion of England. After Evesham Ottobuono did much to ensure the full restoration of royal authority, dominating affairs of both church and state until he left England in 1268.

Edward I did not need papal backing to the same extent as his father had. At the end of his reign, however, he had a helpful ally in the form of Clement V, a Gascon who had once been one of his clerks. It was not hard to persuade Clement to annul the concessions that Edward had been forced to make in 1297. Like Magna Carta in 1215, these were seen as diminishing royal authority, and as having been obtained by coercion. Clement also suspended from office Archbishop Winchelsey, for long a thorn in the royal side.

The support that the crown received from churchmen in England should not be underestimated. Peter des Roches, a Poitevin, great administrator and politician in the early years of Henry III's reign, was bishop of Winchester. Aymer de Valence, half-brother to the king, was a later holder of the same see. Although there was widespread support within the church for Simon de Montfort, the archbishop of Canterbury and the bishops of Hereford, Norwich and Rochester were all royalist in their sympathies. Under Edward I, many bishops were unswerving in their loyalty to the king, and his most important officials held sees. Robert Burnell, bishop of Bath and Wells, was chancellor from 1274 to 1292, and Walter Langton, bishop of Coventry and Lichfield, served as treasurer from 1295 until the end of the reign. Neither man displayed the moral probity expected of a bishop – it was even said that Langton had assisted his mistress in strangling her husband – but both served their dioceses and the king well. Other ministers who combined office with a bishopric included John Kirkby, bishop of Ely, his successor in that see, William of Louth, keeper of the wardrobe, and William March, treasurer and bishop of Bath and Wells. In addition, there was a great increase in the scale of royal patronage within the church at all levels, which brought with it a consequent rise in royal influence.

The church had a traditional role as mediator. When Richard the Marshal rebelled in 1233, a council was held at Westminster. The bishop of Coventry and Lichfield railed against the Marshal, but Edmund of Abingdon, archbishop-elect of Canterbury, intervened with a powerful speech criticising the king's ministers. The outcome was a truce, though this failed to prevent the Marshal's death in Ireland. There are many other examples of churchmen stepping in to try to prevent conflict. In 1297 Anthony Bek, bishop of Durham, irritated his old friend Edward I when he attempted to intervene between the king and his baronial opponents.[5]

The church in England had rights and liberties, which it guarded jealously. When these were threatened, conflict might well arise. The range of potential issues was wide. There were matters such as the right to free, canonical election of bishops, which was threatened by both crown and papacy. Lay taxation of lands held by providing spiritual services was another problem, and there were many difficulties involved in defining ever more closely the problematic boundaries between lay and ecclesiastical jurisdiction. Church reform could never be a purely internal matter, and all too often plans came up against an entrenched royal position.

The development of clerical grievances was complex. One set of complaints would build upon another. The 1250s provide a good example. Difficulties were mounting in the decade. Articles drawn up by Grosseteste, probably in 1253, covered a wide range of issues, including that of how criminal clerks should be dealt with, an issue made famous in the previous century by Thomas Becket. The list concluded with the blunt statement that the king was hardly adhering to any of the clauses of Magna Carta. There was argument over taxation, for the pope had granted Henry III the right to collect a tenth for three years, to be spent on a planned crusade. On 13 May 1253, in the great hall at Westminster, the archbishop of Canterbury, accompanied by thirteen bishops in full regalia, with lighted candles, solemnly issued excommunications against anyone who might transgress the liberties of the church and the free customs of the realm, especially those contained in Magna Carta. This was done in the presence of the king, his brother Richard of Cornwall, Peter of Savoy, and a number of earls and other magnates. Complaints against royal and papal exactions mounted, and in 1257 fifty articles were drafted in convocation, the church's assembly. There were objections to the treatment of the clergy by royal officials, complaints about the treatment of those who took sanctuary in churches, grievances about lay patronage of churches. The liberties of the church were under constant threat, or so it was claimed in highly emotive terms. This threat to the church was an important element in the background to the great events of 1258. These arguments in 1257 do much to explain the support that the baronial reformers received from churchmen in 1258 and the years which followed.[6]

A further element in the situation was Simon de Montfort's own relationship with the church. The one aspect of Simon's career before 1258 which presaged his later role as a reformer was his friendship with the Franciscan Adam Marsh, and the bishop of Lincoln, Robert Grosseteste, a scholar of impressive originality. Montfort borrowed a work from Grosseteste, probably part of a speech the latter made at Rome dealing with the nature of just rule and tyranny. One of Adam's letters praises Earl Simon's plan 'to purify, enlighten and sanctify the Church of God by a government that well benefits it!' Most of the correspondence, however, suggests that the salvation of souls, not the reorganisation of the realm, was what concerned Grosseteste and Marsh.[7]

Whether or not these discussions presaged the reforms of 1258–65, Earl Simon clearly found some inspiration in these ecclesiastical circles. This helps to explain the extraordinary degree of support which he received from the church. He was seen, rightly or wrongly, as a man likely to defend clerical privileges in a way which Henry III had not done. He was able to summon the archbishop of York (Canterbury was absent from the realm), twelve bishops, and a large number of abbots and priors to his partisan parliament early in 1265. The *Song of Lewes* reveals the backing he received from the friars. The bishop of Chichester was one of the three electors appointed after the battle of Lewes: the bishops of Lincoln, London, Winchester and Worcester also provided solid support for the earl. Although some bishops remained royalist, the lower clergy appear to have been largely Montfortian in their sympathies. The miracle cult which developed around Montfort after his death provides further evidence of the importance of religion in explaining the support he received.

The case of the bishop of Worcester's nephew, Thomas Cantilupe, is illuminating. He was of an aristocratic family which had an impeccable tradition of service in the royal household. Thomas, however, went into the church, and was educated at Paris and Oxford, eventually becoming a doctor of canon law. He followed the political example of his uncle, Walter Cantilupe, bishop of Hereford, whose hostility to the crown was based on a resentment of royal and papal exploitation of the church, and on personal friendship with Simon de Montfort. In moving from academic circles at Oxford into the hotbed of Montfortian politics, Thomas was also following the examples of Bishop Berksted of Chichester and Bishop Sandwich of London. Thomas Cantilupe was employed to put the baronial case to Louis IX, in the negotiations which led to the Mise of Amiens in 1264. His scholastic expertise and his previous acquaintance with the French court made him an excellent choice, though his skill in argument did not weigh with Louis, who understandably sided with his fellow monarch, Henry III. In 1265 Cantilupe became chancellor, an office which he appears to have exercised with characteristic application and rigour. Cantilupe's career shows the appeal of the reform movement for intellectuals, and the way in which the dialectic of the schools was transformed into the dialogue of politics. By skill or accident, he left the chancery before the disaster of Evesham. Cantilupe's later career suggests a high measure of political sensitivity. After the civil war he withdrew into academic life, but in 1275 he was elected as bishop of Hereford, and became an important royal councillor to Edward I. At the end of his life he was involved in bitter controversy with the hot-tempered archbishop of Canterbury, Pecham, over a question of the latter's rights of jurisdiction in the see of Hereford. The dispute provides a good illustration of the lack of unity which could affect the church in England. Thomas died in Tuscany, near the papal Curia's summer quarters. His cultivation of large quantities of body lice, and an anti-semitic outburst on the royal council, were among the attributes which led to his eventual sanctification.[8]

Another way in which the church influenced politics under John and Henry III was through the application of crusading ideas and enthusiasm to domestic conflict. With the crusades against the Albigensian heretics in southern France, and against the Hohenstaufen dynasty in Italy and Germany, as well as the crusades in the Baltic region, the movement was no longer limited to expeditions to the Holy Land. Other wars in a holy cause could be given the status of the crusade. In John's reign the Northerners attempted to seize high ground in moral terms when Robert FitzWalter took the title of 'Marshal of the Army of God and Holy Church'. This was emulated by the royalists: in 1217 Philip of Albini was 'Commander of the Militia of Christ'. This approached the status of a crusade, but it was necessary for the papacy to classify a war as a crusade for those fighting in it to gain the full benefits of remission of sins and the protection of the church. The struggle in support of Henry iii in 1216 and 1217 was elevated to the formal status of a crusade by Honorius iii. Indulgences were offered. Even the hardened mercenary Savary de Mauleon took the cross. At the battle of Lincoln the royalists wore white crosses, in part no doubt as a means of recognition, but also to emphasise their crusading status.

Crusading was again in men's minds in the 1260s. One of the charges levied against the king in the hearings before Louis ix at Amiens in 1263 was that he had not fulfilled his crusading vow. It was claimed that his plans to place his second son Edmund on the Sicilian throne meant converting a crusade into an attack on fellow-Christians. Simon de Montfort himself was son of the leader of the crusade against the Albigensian heretics, and was very ready to foster the notion that he was leading a crusade, announcing on one occasion that he had taken the cross, and was as ready to die fighting against wicked Christians for the liberty of the land and church, as against pagans. Bishop Cantilupe of Worcester, who had been authorised to preach a crusade to the Holy Land, promised a crusading indulgence for the king's opponents at Lewes. The royalist emblem of the minority was taken over: white crosses were the Montfortian emblem at Lewes and Evesham.

The royalists had the advantage of papal support when they made use of crusading ideas in the civil war of 1263–5. The papal legates Guy Foulquois and Ottobuono were both empowered to preach the crusade against the rebels. Neither was in a position actually to preach the cross against the Montfortians before Evesham, but the royalists' adoption of red crosses at the battle emphasised their claim to be fighting a holy war against their excommunicated enemies.[9]

There was little danger that the ideology of crusade would be turned against Edward I, the one leader who followed through the Tunis crusade of 1270 with an expedition to the Holy Land. A man of unsophisticated piety, he appreciated the value of support from the church, as is shown by the systematic way he organised prayers for his success in war in the years after 1294.

Yet for all his crusading reputation and his piety, Edward faced continuing arguments over the liberties of the church. Archbishop Pecham of Canterbury, a distinguished scholar, proved a redoubtable opponent. In 1279 he revived old arguments when he had Magna Carta read out in a church council, and issued sentences of excommunication against anyone who might violate its terms, or interfere with church liberties. Pecham had to back down from that challenge, and the weakness of his position was demonstrated by royal legislation in the statute of Mortmain, which forbad the granting of land to the church without royal licence. Further arguments took place in the 1280s. The clergy put forward lengthy grievances in 1285, and appeal was made once more to the principles of Magna Carta. Just as free men should not lose their liberties or free customs without proper judgement, under the terms of clause 39, so should the church's rights and liberties not be despoiled. Vigorous debate was only concluded as a result of the king's desire to end controversy while he was absent from the kingdom visiting the duchy of Gascony from 1286 to 1289.

Much more serious than these disputes was that of 1297, when Edward faced an intransigent archbishop of Canterbury in Robert Winchelsey, and an ambitious and determined pope in Boniface VIII. As part of an initiative to put an end to war between England and France, in 1296 Boniface issued a bull, *Clericis Laicos*, which ordered the clergy not to pay taxes to the lay power. The pope hoped that if the kings of England and France could no longer raise money from the church, they would be unable to fight. Edward had levied an unprecedentedly high tax on the church of half the assessed value of its property in 1294, and had also seized crusading taxes. It is not surprising that Winchelsey chose obedience to the pope rather than to the king: the refusal of the clergy to grant a tax led to their being excluded from the king's protection early in 1297. Clerks had to pay fines, equivalent to the tax they had refused, in order to recover Edward's good grace. Winchelsey's opposition to the king was not fully co-ordinated with that of the earls, but the advantage that the king gained by means of a somewhat artificial reconciliation in July was thrown away by his renewed attempt to tax the clergy in August. Winchelsey was involved in further moves against the king in parliament in 1301, and was accused of weakening the law of the land, disinheriting the crown, and subverting the realm. He ended the reign in exile, but returned under Edward II to provide a measure of inspiration for the authors of the Ordinances of 1311.[10]

A *cause célèbre* in Edward I's last years was his quarrel with his old friend, the powerful bishop of Durham, Anthony Bek. This complex dispute well illustrates the way in which purely ecclesiastical questions could interact with secular affairs. The origins of the dispute lay in Bek's attempt to conduct a visitation of Durham cathedral priory. The monks claimed that they were not subject to such visitations, and a royal attempt to mediate in 1300 met with failure. The intransigence of the bishop was matched by the obstinacy of the priory. The issue was complicated by the fact that the palatinate of Durham was the greatest liberty of the land. Royal officials were excluded from Durham, which was ruled by the bishop and his men. Bek had his own problems in obtaining military service for the Scottish wars from the men of Durham, while the king undoubtedly felt alarm lest the patron saint of Durham, St Cuthbert, whose banner was carried north with the royal armies, might not lend his full support to the campaigns. The result was that on two occasions the palatinate was taken into royal hands. Trust between the king and Bek was broken: only Edward I's death saved the bishop from complete disaster.[11]

A major problem for the church in its incursions into politics was that it was often attempting to fight a war with a popgun. The ceremony of excommunication in Westminster Hall in 1253 was no doubt very splendid, but the king and the lay magnates present promptly made it known that if any additions were made to the sentences of excommunication, they would never consent to them, and would flatly contradict them. Henry III, speaking personally, reserved all the accustomed rights and dignities of the crown and the kingdom.[12] Excommunication was not a powerful weapon. It failed to bring John to heel: it was the political situation which compelled him to come to terms with Innocent III. At the other end of the century, early in 1297, Archbishop Winchelsey excommunicated anyone who disobeyed the terms of the papal bull *Clericis Laicos*. Edward did not ignore this, but counter-attacked. A writ, admittedly of suspect authenticity, from the king forbad the archbishop from taking such action. Itier de Angoulême was appointed to appeal to the pope should Winchelsey take action against the king or any of his officials. Churchmen who threatened officials with excommunication were to be imprisoned. Winchelsey was not to be deterred, and further sentences of excommunication were pronounced in September. A shouting match took place in Canterbury Cathedral itself, when a royal proctor, Hugh of Yarmouth, proclaimed the king's appeal to the pope while Winchelsey was preaching a sermon. No doubt Edward was thoroughly irritated by the threats from the church, but there is little sign that he was in any way diverted from his purpose. It was the failure of his campaign in Flanders, and news that his troops had been defeated in Scotland, that forced Edward to agree to the compromise of the *Confirmatio Cartarum*, not any worries about his spiritual status.[13] The only occasion in this period when a threat of excommunication appears to have been successful was when Edmund of Abingdon threatened Henry III in 1234.

Refusal to grant taxes did not prove to be a very strong weapon for the clergy. Taxation of the church was an important element in royal finances, but the clergy found it hard to take advantage of this. Their position was weakened by the power of the pope to impose taxes for crusading purposes. Some of the receipts from these were then diverted into the royal coffers. Under Henry III the clergy were able to achieve some gains as a result of bargaining over taxation, but Edward I had little patience with them. In 1294 he used the threat of excluding the clergy from his protection to compel them to make a grant of a half the assessed value of their income. In 1297 this threat was put into effect: the great majority of the clergy paid in fines what they would have paid in taxation. The refusal of the clergy to make direct grants to the crown in the last decade of Edward I's reign had little effect, for the king was able to obtain substantial sums from the church out of his share of taxes imposed by the papacy.

Can it be concluded that politics was increasingly secularised in the thirteenth century? This was strongly argued by J. R. Strayer.[14] If this question is answered in simple terms of the number of clerics involved in government and politics, the case is hard to make. Recent study has shown that as early as Henry II's reign about half the judges were laymen, and that it is wrong to imagine that a major change came about when Edward I began to recruit secular professional lawyers to the bench.[15] The career of Edward I's household clerk and administrator John Benstead cannot be used to illustrate the process of laicization. Early in Edward II's reign John abandoned his clerical orders in favour of a secular judicial career, and marriage. However, no one else followed his example. No substantial decline in the proportion of clerics within the royal administration can be discerned in the thirteenth century. Not until Edward III's reign was there to be an anti-clerical reaction to clerical domination of the great offices of state.

It is much harder to determine whether political attitudes became markedly more secular in the course of the century. For Strayer, laicization was linked to an emergent nationalism. Concepts of national sovereignty were increasingly incompatible with ideas of the unity of the Christian world. 'The king and his legitimate orders and instructions, must be fully obeyed by each and every man, great and small, in the realm'.[16] This opening clause of the Dictum of Kenilworth of 1266 was regarded by Strayer as an example of the new spirit of the age.

The pattern of development was surely more complex than this. There was an important ecclesiastical dimension to the great political crises in England throughout the thirteenth century. Innocent III and Stephen Langton made important, if very different, contributions to affairs under John, but it was in the exceptional period from 1258 to 1265 that churchmen and their ideas made their most distinctive mark in political life. Academics such as Thomas Cantilupe were directly drawn in to affairs of state. Crusading concepts were appealed to with some success by both sides in the civil war. The political dialogue, as demonstrated by the *Song of Lewes*, owed much to the debates of the schoolroom. There was no clash between church and state in traditional fashion, but part of the reason why the conflict between the royalists and the Montfortians was elevated from the level of a straightforward power struggle lay in the contribution of churchmen. The political role of the church in these years was surely greater than it had been under King John.

The arguments for the secularisation of politics become stronger by Edward I's reign. The crown was concerned to define the limits of church liberties and rights of jurisdiction, resulting in disputes between church and state. Archbishop Winchelsey's stand against the king was not co-ordinated with the opposition of the earls in 1297. There was little support for the position set out by Boniface VIII in his bull *Clericis Laicos*, forbidding the clergy to pay taxes to the lay power: Edward I's threats were enough to bring most of the church in England to heel, and Winchelsey became increasingly isolated. Crusading ideas were no longer part of the political armoury. To say that politics took a more secular turn does not, however, mean that churchmen no longer had an important role to play. In the mid-1290s the bishops of London, Worcester and Winchester were all regular members of the royal council, and the clergy had their full contribution to make to royal parliaments. Church and state cannot be separated in this period.

5
ENGLISHMEN AND FOREIGNERS

ENGLAND owed much to foreigners in the thirteenth century. Simon de Montfort, the central figure in the baronial opposition movement of Henry III's reign, was a Frenchman. Otto de Grandson, perhaps the most loyal of Edward I's councillors, was from Savoy. The master mason responsible for much of Henry III's rebuilding of Westminster Abbey, Master Henry of Rheims, was probably French, and had certainly learned his trade in France. The magnificent castles built for Edward I in Wales were the work of Savoyard masons and craftsmen, headed by the incomparable Master James of St George. The wars which Edward fought were in part financed by means of loans provided by Italian merchant banking houses, notably the Riccardi of Lucca and the Frescobaldi of Florence. The Italian lawyer, Francesco Accursi, was among the king's advisers who contributed to the work of legal reform. It was a cosmopolitan world.

The immense contribution made by foreigners was not appreciated by contemporaries. Matthew Paris, in the pages of his chronicle, emphasises on many occasions the dislike of aliens, especially those favoured at court. His attitude has not always found favour with later historians. Powicke certainly did not care for it, wishing to see the thirteenth century as an era of internationalism to match the post-war idealism of the period when he wrote. For him, baronial hostility to Henry III's officials did not result from their nationality, but from the fact that household men were taking over the great offices of state. He saw little evidence that the demand for the expulsion of aliens from the realm was a part of the baronial programme in 1258. In dealing with Anglo-French relations under Henry III, he could confidently assert that 'No national feeling lay behind the continuous restlessness of these years'. Historians of a more recent generation, notably Clanchy, Carpenter and Ridgeway, have taken a very different view, and accept the importance of national sentiment in thirteenth-century politics.[1] The issues which concerned people have unfortunately not always been those that historians think they should have been. In the thirteenth century the great questions, in retrospect, may appear to have been those of consent to taxation, the nature of representation, and the control of the crown by means of councils and other mechanisms. In practice, the emotive force of anti-alien movements was a powerful one in the day-to-day politics of the period.

There is no doubt that there were strong national feelings in the thirteenth century. These were more often expressed in terms of a dislike and distrust of other countries, than in terms of national pride. There is much evidence to show that men believed in national stereotypes. The English themselves were widely thought to possess tails. Simon de Montfort said that he had never experienced such infidelity and deception as he had experienced in England, even among the pagans. For the author of the *Life of Edward II*, the English 'excelled all other nations in three qualities, in pride, in craft, and in perjury'. Archbishop Langton commented that the English were 'known everywhere for their incontinence, gluttony and drunkenness'. The Poitevins, so disliked in England, were considered utterly untrustworthy, never keeping their promises, a point made on several occasions in the Life of William the Marshal.[2] They were, at least, not as bad as those who lived further south, in the Pyrenees, whose combination of bestiality and jealousy led them, it was said, to place chastity belts on their mares and mules.[3] Within the

British Isles the Welsh were easily identifiable. During the conquest of Wales by Edward I, Archbishop Pecham found no difficulty in categorising the Welsh as idle, immoral and dishonest, while the king saw them as treacherous and unreliable. Edward I's wars with their associated propaganda did much to fan the flames of national hatred: 'May Scotland be cursed by the mother of God, and may Wales be sunk deep to the devil!' wrote the chronicler Peter Langtoft.[4]

In many ways it is surprising that there should have been any sense of nationality. The aristocracy were French speaking, and there was a popular awareness that they were not English in origin. One chronicler in Edward II's reign criticised the mixed racial origins of the nobles, 'which did not accord well with the kind of blood of England'.[5] Yet by the thirteenth century, the French they spoke was not quite the same as that of France – their accent was evidently strange, and their grammar and vocabulary was, to the ears of a Frenchman, wanting. When a French poet wanted to write an anti-English satire, he made the English nobles speak in bad French, in a mildly obscene manner.[6] It is often immigrant communities that prove the most patriotic, and this may have been the case with the Anglo-Norman aristocracy of England. Men such as the earls of Gloucester and Norfolk could not regard themselves as anything other than *naturales*, native-born Englishmen.

The monarchy helped to foster a sense of Englishness, perhaps in a deliberate attempt to disguise its own Angevin origins. Henry III's cult of Edward the Confessor, after whom he named his eldest son, emphasised the link with Anglo-Saxon monarchy as well as the attraction of a royal saint. In a writ for the collection of scutage in 1235, the king referred to the grant of the tax by 'the earls and barons and all others of our realm of England'.[7] The parliaments that were summoned by Henry III and Edward I were English parliaments, and did not incorporate representatives from the king's other lands. Gascon petitions may have been heard in English parliaments, but Gascon nobles, knights and burgesses did not sit alongside their English counterparts. Ireland had its own parliament. Edward I played the national card in his war propaganda.

The crown certainly had no monopoly of national feeling. A sense of English identity was something to which the king's opponents could and did make effective appeals. Hostility to foreigners was a recurrent theme in the crises of the thirteenth century. In Magna Carta, the expulsion from the realm of Gerard d'Athies, Engelard de Cigogné, Philip Marc and other named foreigners was demanded, as was the removal of all alien knights and mercenaries. In 1258 the barons demanded that heiresses should not be married off to foreigners by the king. Castles should only be entrusted to native-born Englishmen. In parliament, the earl of Norfolk demanded the expulsion of the Poitevins and all aliens from the realm. In Edward I's reign the Jews were expelled from England, and under Edward II it is striking that in the Ordinances of 1311 all the individuals who came under attack – Piers Gaveston, the Frescobaldi bankers, Isabella de Beaumont and her brother Henry – were foreigners. In addition, there was a similar strand of hostility in the church towards foreign clergy who obtained livings in England. In 1245 it was claimed that innumerable Italian clerics were impoverishing the country by exporting its wealth, and that they did nothing to provide pastoral care.[8]

It would be wrong to follow the example of some chroniclers, and treat all aliens alike. In John's reign it was mercenary commanders above all who were disliked, along with those Angevin captains who were retained in the king's service following the loss of Normandy. If the careers of those who are singled out for mention in Magna Carta are analysed, it becomes clear that they were resented for the patronage they received from John, and the political use he made of them. Gerard d'Athies was used against William de Braose in 1208, and then appointed sheriff of Herefordshire. He also received custody of the vacant bishopric of Hereford. Philip Marc was appointed sheriff of Nottinghamshire and Derbyshire in 1208, and retained the office for the rest of the reign. Engelard de Cigogné was sheriff of Gloucestershire and Herefordshire. Fawkes de Breauté was a Norman who established himself in Henry III's minority as sheriff of half a dozen Midland counties and custodian of rather more royal castles. Marriage to the widow of the earl of Devon made him less, not more, acceptable to the English baronage, and in 1224 his power was dramatically broken with the siege of Bedford castle. This followed the radical redistribution of royal castles ordered on the occasion of Henry III's partial majority in 1223. There was a flood of complaints against Fawkes and others, and news that Fawkes's brother had kidnapped a royal justice, Henry de Braybrooke, prompted the use of the feudal host against Bedford. Fawkes was driven into exile.[9]

The most powerful of the Poitevins under King John and in the early part of Henry III's reign was not a military captain, but a bishop and an administrator. Peter des Roches had begun his career in Richard I's household, became bishop of Winchester in 1205, and held the office of justiciar in 1214 and 1215. He it was who had custody of the young Henry during the minority, until his political influence collapsed in 1223–4. He left England on crusade in 1228, and on his return in 1232 rode back to power at the expense of his old rival Hubert de Burgh. Peter des Roches and his nephew (probably a euphemism for son) Peter des Rivaux established themselves in what must have seemed to be a position of unassailable authority. Des Rivaux was at one and the same time treasurer of the household and keeper of the wardrobe and chamber, keeper of the privy seal, and sheriff of no less than twenty-one counties. Many of the names from the past came back to England: notably Engelard de Cigogné and the Poitevin Peter de Maulay. Failure came as a result of the revolt of Richard the Marshal. After the Marshal's murder in Ireland, Henry turned on the Poitevins in a fit of remorse, and removed them from power. Accusations against des Roches and des Rivaux included charges that they 'hated the English nation', and that they had told the king to remove all Englishmen from his household. Peter des

Roches had contradicted the claim that the magnates were entitled to judgement by peers, in accordance with Magna Carta, with the statement that there were no peers in England as there were in France.[10] This further emphasised arguments based on nationality. Anti-alien, or at least anti-Poitevin, sentiment was a significant element in the power struggles of these years.

When writing about the 1250s, Matthew Paris denounced alien influence in England in vehement terms. His indictment was a comprehensive one. The king was said to have lost the affection of the people because of his favours to foreigners, who saw England as easy prey. The Poitevins, in particular, ignored English law, and oppressed the people. It was rumoured that Henry was following the policy of his father, and continuing the feud with the northerners, whose property was being transferred to aliens. On campaign, Englishmen were punished harshly for any offence, aliens only slightly if at all. The church was at the mercy of foreigners. While no Englishmen obtained livings in Italy, Bishop Grosseteste was suspended from his see of Lincoln because he refused to admit to a living an Italian who did not know a word of English. Alien clergy were thought to be in receipt of 70,000 marks a year in rents. The great sees of Canterbury, Hereford and Winchester were in all the hands of foreigners.[11]

These various problems arose largely as a result of the emergence at court of two powerful alien factions, the Savoyards and the Lusignans.[12] Their rise may in part be attributed to Henry's aspirations to cut a figure on the European stage. He may also have felt that the cosmopolitan character of his court added to his prestige and reputation. In a more immediate sense, it was family connections that brought them to England. Henry III married in 1236 Eleanor of Provence, of the house of Savoy. Herself ambitious and determined, she brought in her wake a host of able men, eager to cut out new and profitable careers in England. William, bishop-elect of Valence, the queen's uncle, was promptly appointed to head the king's council, though he did not last long, for he died at Viterbo in 1239. Peter of Aigueblanche, William's clerk, became bishop of Hereford in 1239. Peter of Savoy, another of the queen's uncles, was granted the lands of the earldom of Richmond in 1241, and Boniface of Savoy, another uncle, became archbishop of Canterbury in 1242, and was probably the best-looking man ever to hold that post. Further Savoyards followed, though none were of such distinction. It has been calculated that Henry III gave land to thirty-nine Savoyards in all. Some had important administrative positions in the royal household, the heart of the governmental machine. Peter of Aigueblanche and Artaud de Saint-Romain each held the office of keeper of the wardrobe, Imbert Pugeys and Eble des Montz were among those who served as stewards. The dominant Savoyard at court, however, was not an official, but Peter of Savoy, a great noble and a man of undoubted ability.

The second important, and more sinister, alien group at court was that of the Lusignans from Poitou. They were headed by the king's half-brothers, who came to England in 1247. They were the sons of his mother Isabella and her second husband, Hugh de Lusignan, count of La Marche. Faced with growing French influence in Poitou, particularly following the failure of Henry III's campaign there in 1242, they rightly considered that they had a better chance of finding fame and fortune in England than in France. There were four brothers. William de Valence was married in 1247 to the heiress of the earldom of Pembroke. Aymer was elected to the bishopric of Winchester in 1250, but was not actually consecrated until 1260, the year of his death. There were two younger brothers, Guy and Geoffrey. The Lusignans did not bring as many men in their wake as the Savoyards, but clerks such as Peter Chaceporc played their part in royal administration alongside the Savoyards, and a Poitevin household knight, John de Plessis, was married to the widowed countess of Warwick. The evidence, particularly that of Matthew Paris, suggests that the Poitevins were particularly resented. Their estate officials – ironically mostly Englishmen – were notoriously grasping. There was resentment at the patronage they received. Matthew Paris noted that in 1252 the king refused to allow his own subjects to pay off their debts in instalments, and then gave a grant of land worth 500 marks to a Poitevin, Elye de Raban. The potential for patronage at this period was limited, and the Poitevins found it harder going to secure lands and offices than had the Savoyards. The situation was one of acute tension. Competition for land between Simon de Montfort, who was owed large sums by the king, and William de Valence, presaged future conflict. A number of minor incidents added to Poitevin unpopularity. William de Valence entered a park belonging to the bishop of Ely, and hunted there without permission. He and his men then followed this by ransacking the bishop's manor. At St Albans a messenger sent by Geoffrey de Lusignan made intolerable demands for hospitality, and even asked for all the abbot's horses to be removed from the stables.[13]

The situation was exacerbated by a series of tournaments, in which the aliens of the court took one side, and the native-born baronage the other. The first of these was to have taken place near Dunstable in 1247, but was wisely prohibited by the king. In the following year William de Valence was severely treated at Newbury. Then at Brackley in 1249 the aliens were successful. This conflict was not on purely national lines, for the young earl of Gloucester, no doubt sensing political advantage, sided with the foreigners of the court, an action seen by his compatriots as a clear betrayal. A further tournament was held at Rochester in 1251, in which those defeated at Brackley obtained revenge.[14] In these tournaments all the jealousies of court against country and foreigner against Englishmen found expression.

For those who were not members of the court circle it was natural to regard all the aliens, Poitevin and Savoyard, as the same. In fact the two groups formed very distinct factions, each struggling for power and patronage. Particularly important was the question of control of the heir to the throne, Edward, who by the late 1250s was coming to be of an age where he could expect to play a significant role in affairs of state. No doubt largely through the influence of his mother, Savoyards, along with a few respected Englishmen, had dominated his household. By 1257, however, the Poitevin faction was gaining in influence at the expense of the Savoyards, and the heir to the throne was coming under the influence of his half-uncles, the Lusignans. The situation was a dangerous one.

For historians such as Powicke and Treharne, the Lusignan issue played little part in the early stages of the crisis of 1258. It was considered that it was only at the end of the Oxford parliament in June 1258 that the matter came to the fore, when the brothers' resistance to reform led to their exile from the realm.[15] Carpenter's more recent interpretation sees the initial crisis in 1258 as a movement on the part of a moderate court faction, which included Peter of Savoy, against the unpopular Lusignans. A particular dispute was of prime importance. John FitzGeoffrey, an Englishman, a courtier, and an efficient and loyal servant of the crown, brought a case against Aymer de Valence. Armed retainers of Valence had attacked FitzGeoffrey's servants at Shere in Surrey in the course of a dispute over the advowson there. The king's denial of justice to FitzGeoffrey epitomised the favour accorded to the Lusignans. As Matthew Paris put it, the king had raised up his half-brothers 'as if they had been native born, contrary to the right and law of the kingdom, nor would he allow any writ to go out from the chancery against them'. According to the Tewkesbury chronicle, in the parliament at Westminster held in April 1258 Roger Bigod, earl of Norfolk, demanded the exile of 'the wretched and intolerable Poitevins and all aliens'. In addition to the FitzGeoffrey case, there was a dispute between the earls of Gloucester and Leicester, and William de Valence.[16] Of course, there were many other elements involved in the crisis, notably the king's demand for a grant to finance the extraordinary plan to put his second son Edmund on the Sicilian throne, and the question of the Welsh revolt, but if the Tewkesbury account is accepted, it is clear that hostility to the Lusignans was of prime importance from the outset. Other chroniclers interpreted the crisis in this way. The chronicle of St Benet Hulme provided a short explanation of the origins of the Barons' Wars. The author saw the events exclusively in terms of the rise of the Poitevins, and explained that native-born Englishmen were virtually disinherited, for no justice could be obtained against them. The fourteenth-century St Albans chronicler, John Trokelowe, considered that the question of the aliens was the prime cause of the dissension between the king and the barons. After the Westminster parliament the general issues of how the realm should be governed were thrashed out in the Oxford parliament in June. When debate turned to individuals, it was the king's Lusignan half-brothers who were attacked and driven into exile: they, above all, were held responsible for all that had gone wrong in the years leading up to the crisis. Although it was the Poitevins in particular who came under attack, all aliens were blackened with the same brush. According to the arbitration made by Louis IX in 1264, the Mise of Amiens, a statute was made 'declaring that the realm of England should in future be governed by native-born men, and that aliens must depart, never to return, save those whose stay the faithful men of the realm might in common accept'. As no text of the original enactment survives, its date is not known, but 1258 seems very likely.[17]

Anti-alien feelings continued as one element among the many cross-currents in the complex manoeuvres of the period of baronial reform and rebellion. In his trial in 1260, Simon de Montfort claimed of the king that 'it seemed that he put his trust more in foreigners than in the men of his own land'. Grievances drawn up in 1264 stressed the harm done by alien courtiers and nobles. According to one account, just before civil war began in the same year, an embassy of bishops was sent by the barons to the king. They offered to accept the conditions of the Mise of Amiens, provided that Henry III would agree to the exile of aliens and agree that the country should be governed by native-born men. Such a condition was unacceptable. The *Song of Lewes* included the familiar complaint that the king called in foreigners, to whom the kingdom was subjected. Escheats and wardships went to them, not Englishmen. In contrast, David, Moses and Solomon had relied upon their own people. In the *Forma Regiminis*, the arrangement made for the government of the country after the battle of Lewes, it was laid down that the three electors, the nine councillors, and all castle constables, together with other royal bailiffs, should all be natives.[18]

This insistence on government by Englishmen raises the question of how contemporaries could equate such a programme with the leadership of a foreigner, Simon de Montfort. Montfort-l'Amaury is in the Île-de-France, and Simon's upbringing was wholly French. His family possessed a claim to the earldom of Leicester, but when he first came to England and married the king's sister, he must have seemed to be yet another foreign adventurer. Nor was Simon a man to hide the fact that he despised the English, as witness his boast on the eve of his death at Evesham, that it was he who had taught them to advance in good order. His quarrels with the king must have done much to render him acceptable, and although he was French, he was neither a Poitevin nor a Savoyard. Even so, a propaganda letter included in the Tewkesbury annals, clearly written in the interest of the earl of Gloucester, noted that while Montfort persecuted some foreigners, he favoured others. His own foreign origins were not forgotten. For many he was the one man to remain consistently faithful to the principles of the Provisions of Oxford, but for others, he was an unscrupulous foreigner taking advantage of the situation in England to pursue his personal ambitions.[19]

The triumph of the royalists at the battle of Evesham was not a victory for the aliens who had been so fiercely attacked at the outset of years of crisis, back in 1258. It was, rather, a triumph for Prince Edward and the allies he had found among the lords of the Welsh marches. None the less, the victory at Evesham meant that the aliens could return to England. Boniface of Savoy, archbishop of Canterbury, and Peter of Aigueblanche, the hated bishop of Hereford, came back. William de Valence returned, and although he never received the title of earl of Pembroke, he played a major role in English affairs until his death in 1296. A substantial number of Savoyard and Poitevin families recovered the lands they had been given in England.[20]

Hostility to foreigners did not continue to be a political issue under Edward I as it had been under his father. The king did not adopt a policy of exclusively favouring native-born Englishmen, but his patronage of foreigners was not so aggressive as had been the case under Henry III. Edward's position was easier. His queens, first Eleanor of Castile and then Margaret of France, did not bring a host of greedy followers with them to England in the way that Eleanor of Provence had done. The king had no acquisitive half-brothers whose desire for land had to be accommodated. When, at the end of the reign, Edward granted his favourite nephew, John of Brittany, the earldom of Richmond, and followed this by making him royal lieutenant in Scotland, he was in a position of such power that no opposition was likely. Also, John had a family claim to the earldom, and was not personally offensive in the way that the Lusignans had been. When Edward granted land to his Savoyard councillor, Otto de Grandson, it was in Ireland and the Channel Isles, and so there was no threat to English landholding interests. The foreign knights who served in Edward's household normally received rewards in cash rather than in land. When a foreigner who was also, to make matters worse, a woman, was granted Bamburgh castle, the king carefully distanced himself from the grant. The treasurer, Walter Langton, was left to bear the responsibility.[21] Indeed, rather than allow his opponents to employ the anti-alien argument, Edward made emotive use of it in his own propaganda in his wars. In a celebrated writ in 1295 he claimed that the French were intending to eradicate the English tongue from the land. The term 'tongue' implied nation, as well as language.[22]

In the difficult initial years of Edward II's reign, the old arguments began to surface again. The extraordinary scale of the favours granted by the inept king to his favourite, Piers Gaveston, would have caused problems had Piers been an Englishman, but the fact that he was a Gascon undoubtedly exacerbated matters. There were not, however, the host of foreigners battening upon England that there had been under Henry III. As well as demanding Gaveston's expulsion from the realm, the Ordainers asked for the removal of Henry de Beaumont and his sister Isabella de Vescy, together with that of the Florentine royal bankers, the Frescobaldi. While xenophobic sentiments no doubt played their part in these demands, this was not an anti-alien movement as such. It was particular individuals who were attacked, not foreigners in general.

Other aspects of English hostility to aliens in the thirteenth century did not have as much political importance as the movement against the Poitevins in Henry III's reign. The Jews were an alien group in English society, distinctive in religion, dress and language. Their role as moneylenders, and their religion, rendered them unpopular. One of Simon de Montfort's earliest actions in England was to expel the Jewish community from his town of Leicester, on the grounds that Christians suffered from their usurious activities. Debts owed to the Jews themselves were not as significant politically as the attitude taken by the crown towards collection of those debts when a Jewish creditor died, and the crown acquired the right to them. The question of these debts came to the fore in 1212, when King John offered to relax the demands made by the crown for repayment, in a move clearly intended to defuse the situation caused by the baronial plot against him.[23] In 1215 the barons demanded protection for widows and children in cases where landowners were indebted to Jews, or where a Jewish debt had come into the hands of the crown. The matter of Jewish debts was brought up again in 1258. The Jews were, of course, of great value to the crown. Regarded as royal chattels, they were subject to arbitrary taxation. A 20,000 mark tallage in 1241–2, and one of 60,000 marks three years later, testified to the wealth of the Jewish communities in England. Yet taxation at such a rate crippled those communities. By Edward I's reign, receipts from the Jews fell to very low levels. The last tax on them raised little more than £4,000. In 1290 the king willingly agreed to their expulsion from the realm, as part of the package which saw the grant in parliament of a tax which raised some £118,000.[24]

Other financiers did not attract the same degree of hostility as did the Jews, though there was a complaint in the Petition of the Barons of 1258 against Christian usurers, and the Cahorsins from southern France in particular. It was in practice the Italian merchant bankers who played an increasingly significant role both in trade and in crown finance during the thirteenth century. Under Edward I first the Riccardi and then the Frescobaldi lent massively to the crown in return for promises of revenue from the customs, and various privileges. The great Italian firms came to control much of the English wool export trade, and were much used by great landowners as financial agents. They were undoubtedly unpopular, particularly when over-extended companies failed to meet their financial obligations, but it was not until Edward II's reign that Italian bankers became politically significant. It was then that opposition to the Frescobaldi was openly expressed. Edward, in contrast to his father, had been lavish in the grants he made to the Italians, one of whom was given a place on the royal council. There were understandable suspicions since they had not accounted properly at the exchequer for the money they had received from the customs, and in 1311 they were expelled from the realm. This, however, was simply a move against one company, and was not directed at the entire Italian community in England. It should be seen as a criticism of the financial methods initiated by Edward I and continued by his son, and not as part of a wider move against all Italians or all aliens.[25]

Foreign involvement in the English church was a matter of increasing concern in the thirteenth century. The development by the papacy of its rights to 'provide' or appoint clergy to livings resulted in the nomination of Italian and other clerics to positions in England. The monastery of Ramsey complained in 1228 that nearly a quarter of its revenues were being paid out to papal provisors, and while the total number of foreigners appointed to English livings cannot be calculated, it was certainly considerable. In the majority of cases papal provisors did not take up residence, but took the revenues of English churches, leaving a low-paid vicar to carry out their duties. There was a widespread campaign in England, led by a knight called Robert Twenge, in 1232: foreign ecclesiastics and their property were attacked. Twenge was aggrieved because an Italian had been appointed to a church over which he claimed rights of patronage. No less a person than Hubert de Burgh was accused of being implicated in the riots; this charge led to his fall from power. Later, in 1239, Twenge's complaints against papal provisors led to the presentation of a formal appeal to the papacy by the English magnates. The question was one which concerned the barons in 1258–9: they were naturally anxious to defend their own rights to ecclesiastical patronage. Intermittent protests against foreign clergy continued. In 1305 the community of the realm petitioned the king about the way in which monastic houses were impoverishing the country, by sending money to their mother-houses overseas. A statute dealing with this was promulgated at the Carlisle parliament of 1307, a parliament which also witnessed vehement protests against the papal tax-collector, William Testa.[26] The continuing perceived problem of foreign clergy was not, perhaps, of great political moment. It was not a matter on which the king and his subjects were sharply divided. It was, however, another element which added to the general unpopularity of foreigners.

It would be wrong to see xenophobic attitudes as a prime cause of the political problems of the thirteenth century, but it would be equally wrong to deny the importance of national feelings. There was no question of automatic hostility to all aliens, but if there were grievances against foreigners, the very fact of their being foreign helped to focus those grievances. Simon de Montfort was an alien, but was accepted because he had a justified claim to the earldom of Leicester, and did not long remain in favour with the king. The king's Poitevin relations, and to a lesser extent the Savoyards who followed the queen to England, were seen as a threat to established landed interest in England. The behaviour of the Poitevins was such that they were seen as also threatening English law, liberty and custom. It was easy for their opponents to use the argument of nationality against them. Men could identify themselves more easily with hostility to aliens, than with the higher ideals of the reform of the realm. There is also no doubt that the disputes between the Poitevin and Savoyard factions at court in the 1250s contributed much to the growing crisis, and that the question of the king's Lusignan half-brothers was a catalyst at the Westminster parliament of 1258. Foreigners may have contributed much in a positive way towards the development of England in the thirteenth century, but contemporaries such as Matthew Paris were not wrong to see them as a dangerous and divisive force.

6

MILITARY SERVICE

WAR WAS a potent factor in thirteenth-century politics. King John's failure to retain Normandy in 1204, and the defeat of his allies at Bouvines in 1214 were major steps on the road to Runnymede and the final crisis of the reign. Had Henry III been successful in his campaigns in France in 1230 and 1242, or achieved more on his Welsh expeditions, he would have faced far fewer problems at home. The crisis of 1297 was very largely the result of the immense burden that Edward I had imposed on the country since 1294, with campaigns against the Welsh, Scots and French. The difficulties of Edward's final years, and those of his son's reign, have to be seen against the sombre background of the Scottish wars of independence.

England was affected by war in various ways. Direct experience of devastation and slaughter was limited. It came chiefly with civil war, notably at the end of John's reign, and in 1264–5. Foreign invasion took place at the outset of Henry III's reign, with the French prince Louis's intervention, and with Scottish raids at the end of the period. Much more important in political terms were the problems of raising the men, money and materials for the various expeditions mounted by the English. The consequent burden on the country was very considerable. Success in war might make this acceptable: failure led to resentment. For those of the laity most influential in political affairs, the earls and barons, the question of military service was close to their hearts.

The aristocratic society of the thirteenth century was warlike. The central ideals were chivalric: the skills that were highly valued were those of fighting with lance and sword on horseback. If there were no wars to be fought, then tournaments might provide a somewhat safer and more convenient substitute. At the same time, this was a period of crisis for English armies. The costs of warfare rose sharply in the late twelfth and early thirteenth centuries. Where it had been possible to obtain the services of a knight for 8 *d*. a day, it was now necessary to spend 2 *s*. Equipment was becoming more elaborate and expensive: war-horses were more costly. Ultimately the authority of the state depended on the military strength that it could muster. The crown had traditional rights to call for feudal military service from its tenants-in-chief, but the nature and scale of those rights were bound to be questioned. The king's greater subjects may have been eager to prove their reputations on the field of battle, but they were equally eager to defend their rights against what they saw as unacceptable demands for their service. The nature of the service that they could provide was undergoing a major transformation in response to the changing nature of baronial authority. It was with cavalry service alone that the magnates were concerned: the recruitment of infantry was not of great political significance. Nor did the question of military service bulk equally large in all the political crises of this period: it was John and Edward I who were seen as making unacceptable demands in this matter on their subjects, rather than Henry III. Nor is it a matter which features extensively in the documents thrown up by the various political crises, for reasons which need to be explained.

The conventional view is that the thirteenth century witnessed the decline of traditional forms of feudal military service, and that the crown developed alternatives which were used to formidable effect by Edward I in his wars in Wales and Scotland. There were new ideas about military obligation, with the development of the concept that all those who fitted a specific wealth qualification should become knights, and the crown was able to make use of paid troops on an increasing scale. The development of contracts is seen as important in this process.[1]

The issue which proved most contentious was not whether the crown was entitled to demand service, or the scale of that service, but where the service was to take place. In 1213 John's plans for an expedition to France aroused such hostility that he had to abandon them. Early in the following year he demanded the feudal service of his tenants-in-chief for a campaign in Poitou. A significant group, largely of northern barons, refused to participate or even to send men with the king. They would not even pay scutage in lieu of service when this was demanded later in the year. There were various possible grounds for this refusal: some Northerners had reasons for claiming that they were obliged by the terms of their tenure to serve only against the Scots. The most important argument, however, was that put in the so-called Unknown Charter which preceded Magna Carta itself. According to this document, there was to be no service overseas save in Normandy and Brittany. There were presumably sufficient precedents from the Norman past to warrant service there: what was objected to was service in the Angevin lands, and perhaps also service in Ireland.[2]

It is hard to determine how deeply men were aggrieved by the request to serve in Poitou. It is likely that John's opponents, such as Eustace de Vesci, were seeking an issue on which to confront the king, and this was a convenient one. A refusal to fight or to co-operate over the campaign could hit the king's plans hard. At the same time, there is no doubt that John's demands for service had been considerable. In particular, the scutages which followed the feudal summonses were a substantial financial burden. Yet when it came to the attempt to settle the crisis, in Magna Carta itself, the question of feudal service did not feature largely. Clause 16 declared that no one was to be compelled to perform more service from a knight's fee than was due, but such a general statement could hardly begin to deal with the specific questions that had been raised in 1213 and 1214. It is very curious that the issue which had been so much to the fore at the onset of the crisis was barely even dealt with when a settlement of sorts was agreed, particularly since it had been dealt with in the Unknown Charter. In part this may have been because by 1215 the issue was no longer so important: the defeat of John's allies at Bouvines in 1214 had spelled the end of his continental ambitions. In part, too, it must be suspected that the crown was very reluctant indeed to make formal concessions on so important an issue as that of military service.

Henry III mounted military expeditions abroad on three occasions, in 1230, 1242, and 1253. On the first occasion there was remarkably little opposition to the government's plans. In part this may have been because the campaign was mounted on a fairly small scale; in addition, it may have been more acceptable because the initial landing was made in Brittany, even though the fighting, such as it was, took place in Poitou. In 1242, however, the king faced much greater problems with his subjects. Again the campaign was to take place in Poitou. The bishops claimed exemption from military service abroad, and the response of the secular tenants-in-chief was very limited. No doubt because of their opposition, the actual form of summons used in 1242 did not demand the provision of feudal service, but instead the great men were asked, in effect, to provide appropriate contingents. An attempted inquiry into knight service which followed a disastrously inadequate muster had to be abandoned. Yet the great earls were prepared to serve, and the campaign did take place, though it proved embarrassingly ineffective.[3] In 1253 Henry III feared an invasion of Gascony from Castile. In the event no such invasion took place, and although the summons of the feudal host did take place, there was a rapid realisation in England that no campaign was in fact necessary. The incident was more significant as the occasion for a request for taxation, than in terms of the demand for service. Nevertheless, the army the king took to Gascony was far from being negligible in size. These expeditions under Henry III show the problems the crown faced in obtaining service for campaigns which did not attract widespread support: at the same time, it does not appear that the king's demands provoked fierce hostility from his greater subjects.

For the rest of Henry's reign the king was in no position to request military service, save when he needed to raise troops in the difficult situation of civil war in the mid-1260s. Military service was not a significant issue in the great crisis of 1258. With the ambitious and far more warlike Edward I on the throne, however, the story would be a different one.

Demands for military service in Edward's Welsh wars were not a cause of political dissension. There were problems in 1282, when the king initially chose not to employ a traditional type of feudal summons, preferring to recruit a paid army, but it seems that, after protests, he abandoned his plans. It was service abroad, not service within the British Isles, that would cause difficulties. There were signs of impending trouble in 1294, with the use of a feudal summons to recruit troops for Gascony, but news of revolt in Wales put paid to the king's plans. The crisis came in 1297, when Edward planned to send one army to Gascony, and to take a force himself to fight in Flanders. The plan aroused protests in parliament at Salisbury from the earl of Norfolk, Roger Bigod. Neither he, as marshal, nor Humphrey de Bohun, as constable, would co-operate with a muster in June at London. This was the product of an unorthodox writ of summons, which did not appeal to the traditional obligations resulting from fealty and homage. An offer of pay to those who were prepared to go with the king did little to improve the situation, and in the end Edward sailed with little more than the troops provided by his own household. This row over military service was one element among many in a complex political crisis – taxation, lay and ecclesiastical, and demands for food supplies were among the others – but it was a very important one. There were strong echoes of 1214 in the baronial claim that no service was owed in Flanders: neither the barons nor their ancestors had ever performed feudal service there. Yet just as in 1215, in the settlement of the crisis of 1297 which came in the *Confirmatio Cartarum*, the issue of military service was not resolved. As in John's reign, it was the case that with the campaign effectively over, the issue was perhaps no longer urgent, but it must be suspected that this was a matter on which the king was simply not prepared to yield.

The Scottish wars of Edward I's final years were not without argument over military service, even though there was broad support for the king's aims. One element in 1297 of great importance had been the king's attempt to extend the liability to service to all those who possessed at least £20 worth of land a year. In 1300 he attempted something similar, although this time the level was set at £40 a year. There was a protest at this in a draft statement of grievances, although in the eventual *Articuli super Cartas* which the king conceded, the clause was removed. Yet he did not repeat a summons to the £40 landholders as such, although in 1301 these men – over 900 of them – were all sent individual requests that they come to fight in Scotland. Hostility to such innovations meant a reversion to traditional means of summons for the last campaigns, with feudal summonses in 1303 and 1306. In 1311, however, the Ordinances included a clause which stated that the king should not go abroad, or make war, without the consent of the baronage in parliament. This had immediate reference to Edward II's transparent tactic of diverting attention away from political troubles at home by launching a campaign against the Scots, but it surely also looked back to Edward I's unpopular and unwise expedition to Flanders. The clause is a very important one, representing the first clear limitation on the king's power to make war, and with it to demand military service.[4]

The question of military service was much more complex than simply that of whether or not the king had the right to ask for men to follow him on campaigns overseas. The changing character of service influenced the way the arguments went, with the period seeing a decline in formal baronial obligation, and attempts by the crown to establish a more general duty to serve.

In 1166 Henry II had ordered the one full-scale inquiry

into feudal service that ever took place in medieval England. The total number of knights due from the tenants-in-chief was approximately 5,300. Some great men owed huge quotas: the honour of Clare alone was assessed at $127\frac{1}{4}$ fees. It is doubtful whether the full service was ever demanded by Henry II, who in 1157 asked for one-third of the total, and two years later preferred to take scutage, money in lieu of service, from the bulk of his tenants-in-chief. Yet feudal service was not abandoned: it was requested for Ireland in 1171, for an expedition to Galloway in 1186, and at the end of the reign for a campaign in France. By John's reign, if not earlier, the king had to be content, not with the full quotas of the 1166 survey, but with men coming on campaign accompanied by a retinue appropriate to their standing. For the Irish expedition of 1210 Geoffrey FitzPeter provided a mere ten knights, not the full quota of almost a hundred that was his formal obligation. In the Poitou campaign of 1214, the earl of Devon served with twenty knights, whereas he was due to produce no less than eighty-nine. This reduction in the old feudal quotas continued, to be effectively completed by the time of the Welsh campaign of 1245.

This reduction in feudal quotas was not the result of any one single crisis, yet it represented a major change in the relationship between the crown and the baronage. It was forced on the crown by economic circumstances, but it went much further than was necessary. A muster roll shows that in 1229 the greatest earls were expected to provide no more than twenty knights each; most tenants-in-chief were asked for a mere one, two or three. Another roll, from 1245, shows that the process of reduction of quotas was more or less complete by then. Grants made in this period show a startling fall in the crown's military demands. When Richard, earl of Cornwall, was granted the honour of Wallingford, he was obliged to provide merely three knights, whereas the old obligation stood at 100. He received Cornwall for the service of five knights: the old assessment was 215. These numbers were far below the true military capabilities of the great men of the realm.

The various armies were not all summoned in the same way. In some cases the crown specifically asked for reduced quotas: in others it demanded the *servitia debita*, the traditional service due from the tenants-in-chief. In practice, however, it does not appear that the response was very different. The barons very understandably seized on the lowest level of service the crown requested, and treated that as a precedent to be followed for the future. Many reductions must, of course, have been achieved by means of a process of individual bargaining on an *ad hoc* basis. There was no universal percentage by which the old quotas were reduced: it was, presumably, largely a matter of what tenants-in-chief could get away with. In nearly all cases the answer was a great deal. The overall result of the reductions in quotas was that the troops the crown might expect to muster in response to a feudal summons numbered perhaps some 600 knights in the early thirteenth century. By 1245 it was possible to send two mounted sergeants in lieu of one knight, and in the 1277 army Edward I had a total feudal service of 228 knights and 294 sergeants. Records are not complete for all armies, though the last but one feudal muster to take place in England, that of 1322, yielded a force of about 500 men, almost all sergeants. Not only were numbers relatively low: these feudal forces were obliged to serve only for a period of forty days, a severe limitation.[5]

The reductions only applied to service in the field, not to the fiscal obligations of tenants-in-chief. The exchequer did not adjust its records to take account of the military changes, and demands for scutage continued to be issued as in the past, based on the full number of fees recorded. This frequently resulted in argument, as the exchequer by Edward I's reign was demanding scutage on the grounds that full service had not been performed, whereas the tenants-in-chief claimed that they had fulfilled their obligations by going to fight with the new reduced quotas. Yet even with this qualification, there can be little doubt that the baronage had achieved a major triumph in bringing down a major obligation to a level which was little more than nominal.

If the crown had relatively few troops at its disposal recruited by feudal means, what could it do? There was the royal household, with its retained knights. The number of these men varied considerably through the period, but in the late 1230s and early 1240s Henry III retained about seventy-five knights each year. In the mid-1280s Edward I had over 100, though the number was much lower by the end of the reign when financial pressures were more acute. These household knights formed the backbone of the army. Some would bring their own followers with them on campaign, and in time of need the royal household could be expanded very substantially. Over 500 cavalry were provided by the household for the Flanders campaign in 1297, with more than 300 being temporarily retained in addition. The household provided some 800 cavalry for the 1298 campaign in Scotland.

This was not sufficient to meet the crown's military ambitions. Various attempts were made to establish a new system of military obligation. In 1224, for the first time, orders were issued that all laymen who held at least one knight's fee should become actual knights. This was probably associated with plans for an expedition to France, but as this did not take place, the measure had little effect. In December 1241, however, a new distraint was ordered. This time, it was not only those who possessed at least a knight's fee, but all those who had lands worth at least £20 a year who were to become knights. Soon, it was made clear that all knights were expected to take part in the king's Poitou campaign. In 1253 similar measures were taken. All those with £20 worth of land were to become knights, or to pay fines in lieu. There was evidently much opposition. Many tenants-in-chief refused to respond to the summons to muster at Portsmouth, and a relaxation of the financial limit from £20 to £30 does not appear to have had much effect. After the king had sailed, all those who had not co-operated were ordered to appear before the council, but there was little that could be done. A chronicle reported that in the next year, 1254, all £10 landholders were distrained, and asked to muster along with the magnates. A report from the regents in England to the king indicated that the earls and barons were prepared to go to fight against Alphonso of Castile, but it was feared that others would not go, unless the most solemn undertakings to maintain the terms of Magna Carta were made. In fact, as already shown, Gascony was not attacked by Alphonso, and Henry III had no need of a substantial army there. It was not necessary to try to enforce to the full the measures that had been instituted, and distraint of knighthood could be used as a convenient means of raising fines from those who did not choose to be knighted, rather than being employed as a means of compelling men to fight at the king's bidding. As the measures were not carried through to their full logical conclusion, so opposition to them was, in the end, limited and partial. However, the crown's power to introduce innovations in the system of military service had at the same time been shown to be limited.[6]

The precedents set under Henry III were not forgotten, though Edward I had no real need to turn to them in the course of his Welsh wars, when recruitment was not a major problem. In 1283, however, assemblies of £20 landholders were held at Northampton and York: this was with the intention of obtaining financial support from those who were not participating in the campaign. In 1295, during the Welsh revolt, orders were sent out instructing the sheriffs to draw up lists of £30 landholders. These men were to be ready to set out on campaign, fully equipped, at three weeks' notice. They were promised pay in return, should they be needed. In 1296 the level was set at £40, but in the difficult circumstances of 1297 the sheriffs were asked to draw up lists of £20 landholders. These men were ordered to muster at London, ready for the campaign overseas. The measure was successful only in so far as lists were actually drawn up, but of the 713 names in those that have survived, only seventy-six actually appear to have sailed to Flanders. These attempts to widen the basis of military obligation ran into massive passive resistance. Despite this failure, Edward I again had lists of £40 landholders drawn up in 1300, and this class of men was duly summoned, with an offer of wages, to fight in Scotland.

There were protests, but no formal concession was made by the crown, and in the following year the lists were used to summon 935 men individually to go on the royal campaign.[7] That marked the end of these experiments. During the thirteenth century the crown had attempted to extend the notion of military obligation beyond the traditional duty owed by the tenants-in-chief, aiming to introduce a wealth qualification. There is an obvious parallel with taxation, where national systems of assessment were introduced to replace feudal forms of tax. There the crown was successful: in the military field it was not.

If the crown could not establish new systems of military obligation, one alternative was to rely on paid troops, in addition to those retained as household knights. There would have been nothing new in this. Such means had been more important in recruiting eleventh and twelfth century English armies than the use of feudal musters. There was a long tradition of employing mercenaries, but this was not only increasingly expensive, but also extremely unpopular. John made extensive use of mercenaries, who were mostly recruited in the Low Countries. Their use was widely criticised: the papacy had condemned such men in the Third Lateran Council of 1279. From the point of view of the English barons, there was an obvious threat to their own authority should the crown develop its power further on such a basis. It is hardly surprising that the expulsion of all foreign mercenaries was demanded in Magna Carta, along with that of specific named captains. Thereafter mercenaries recruited abroad were not much used in England. Prince Edward attracted much criticism when he returned to England in 1263 with a troop of foreign mercenary knights. When he became king, Edward did employ a few foreigners as household knights, but these men were hardly mercenaries in the normal sense of the word.

An alternative to using foreign mercenaries was, of course, for the king to pay his own subjects for their service. As has been seen, offers of pay were indeed made to those whom the king attempted to summon in accordance with a wealth qualification. In the early part of this period magnates certainly accepted pay from the crown. William the Marshal's accounts for 1193 show that he received royal pay for the troops under his command, and again, in the period following John's death, he did not meet the costs of his knights and other soldiers out of his own pocket. There is no evidence that he was paid wages personally, but the earl of Salisbury certainly received an annual fee from King John.[8]

With the reduction in the feudal quotas, some tenants began to provide on a voluntary basis service in addition to what was formally expected of them. In 1245 Roger de Quincy, earl of Winchester, appeared with ten knights, but claimed that his quota was only three and a half. Summonses would ask not merely for the *servitium debitum*, the service owed, but also for such additional troops as could be raised. By Edward I's reign attitudes were very different from those of the early thirteenth century. In 1282 the earls of Hereford and Gloucester, and perhaps others, refused to accept wages, preferring to fight at their expense. It may be that they considered that taking wages placed them at the king's beck and call, and reduced their own authority. Thereafter, Edward I could not persuade his earls to serve for pay. He was therefore all the more dependent on their goodwill, and one result was the absence of the earls from his ineffectual campaign in Flanders in 1297. It appears likely that on such campaigns as that of 1298, when the Scots were defeated at Falkirk, or 1300 when Caerlaverock castle was taken, about two-thirds or even three-quarters of the cavalry in the English army were serving on a voluntary basis.[9] This did not mean that service went unrewarded. Those who fought for the king expected to receive grants of lands and other favours from him, and they shared in the benefits of royal protection that were customarily accorded to those who fought. This meant that their lands were safe from legal action during their absence.

As far as the cavalry was concerned, pay under Edward I was largely confined to the forces permanently or temporarily attached to the royal household. There was, however, one significant exception to the unwillingness of the earls to accept pay. They were ready to take the king's money if they fought in places where or at times when they did not consider service to be customary. Campaigns in Gascony, and expeditions to Scotland in the winter, did see magnates accepting pay, sometimes on a contractual basis. The use of contracts offering pay was a familiar feature of English fourteenth-century armies, notably of those that fought in France, but this practice was uncommon under Edward I, and should not be seen as an element in the transformation of the system of military service. Contracts, of course, were extensively used by the great men to retain knights and others in their service, but where the crown paid troops, it preferred to account precisely for the numbers serving, rather than to engage with commanders to provide men in return for a lump sum. Only in cases where the administrative machinery was not available to pay wages on a regular basis were contracts employed: thus we find them used when Edward sent troops to fight in Gascony in the 1290s, and when forces were despatched to Scotland at a time when the king and his household administrative staff were in Flanders, in the winter of 1297–8.

Infantry service did not provoke political argument, for the common footsoldier lacked the influence of the social élites, who fought on horseback with sword and lance. Under Edward I an elaborate system for recruiting infantry by means of commissions of array was developed. The government was capable of mustering up to 30,000 footsoldiers for a single campaign, though there were very considerable problems of desertion to be faced once the men had assembled. These men were all paid by the crown, and although it is far from clear what rights the crown had to compel them to go on campaign, there was little argument over this issue. There is evidence of resentment at a village level of the activities of the royal commissioners of array, but the bewildered ordinary peasant unwillingly forced into the ranks had no means to express his opposition to what was taking place.[10]

Military service does not feature in the forefront of the documents thrown up by the political crises of the thirteenth century, largely because this was a question on which the crown was unwilling to make formal concessions. This did not mean that there was no change in the system. On the contrary, there were very significant changes, and these were of considerable political importance. The king's greatest subjects, his tenants-in-chief, succeeded in reducing their formal obligations to the crown to a level where they did not represent a major burden. This was achieved quietly, rather than at a single blow. It shifted the balance of power within the realm. The crown was unable to establish an effective alternative system of service, and became increasingly reliant on the voluntary backing provided by the nobility. The use of pay was not new in this period, and it did not provide the crown with an effective alternative means of gaining military, and with it political, power and authority. The voluntary co-operation of the magnates in any military venture was essential. The limitations on the king were not a severe handicap as far as wars in Wales and Scotland were concerned, for there were sufficient men with a vested interest to ensure that recruitment was not a major problem. Where war overseas was concerned, however, the period began with the refusal of some magnates to fight for John in Poitou, and near the end of it Edward I was faced by the refusal of many of his subjects, greater and lesser, to go to fight in Flanders. In the Ordinances of 1311 the king's power to make war and go overseas was limited, and subjected to baronial assent, almost a century after the issue had been raised by the Northerners under King John.

7
TAXATION

THE POLITICAL importance of taxation appears self-evident. The process of obtaining grants has usually involved complex bargaining, with the crown offering to remedy grievances in exchange for the funds it required. Yet historians have put forward very different views about taxation in this period. For some, such as S. K. Mitchell and J. G. Edwards, the position appeared relatively straightforward. The traditional feudal sources of revenue were, by the thirteenth century, insufficient. New taxes, notably those levied on an assessment of personal wealth, were needed. To obtain grants, collective, corporate consent was far more satisfactory than personal consent. The most convenient method was to ask for grants from the magnates together with representatives of shires and boroughs in parliaments. Taxes could be refused as well as granted, and as a result a political dialogue took place.

A very different view was advocated by Gaines Post, and developed by G. L. Harriss. This stressed the importance of new ideas drawn from Roman law. It was not practical politics and financial need that led the king to seek consent for his taxes, but a legal imperative. The notions of representation drew on the concepts and terminology of Roman law. Also derived from Roman law was the doctrine of necessity. If there was a state of urgent necessity, such as a threat of invasion, the king was entitled to receive aid from his subjects. They were obliged to provide taxes, although he was still bound to obtain their consent. The political implications of the two approaches are very different. If requests for taxation were seen in a purely pragmatic way, then negotiation was very much a matter of practical politics. Reforms could be obtained in return for grants. If, however, the argument all took place within a framework of Roman law, the potential for using taxation as a means of obtaining concessions from the king was very much less.[1]

The reasons for imposing taxes were simple. The crown's revenues from lands and other traditional sources, such as the profits of justice, were insufficient to meet the rising costs that it faced during this period. By feudal custom, reasserted in Magna Carta in its 1215 version, the king could only levy taxes to pay for his own ransom, the knighting of his eldest son, and the marriage of his eldest daughter. The years from about 1180 witnessed a sharp rise in prices, and although the period of inflation is normally considered to have lasted until about 1220, prices in fact continued to rise steadily during the thirteenth century. Knightly wages were an important element in the costs of war: as has been seen, they rose from 8 *d.* a day under Henry II to 2 *s.* a day by John's reign. During the Barons' Wars even higher rates were sometimes paid. Costs of foodstuffs for armies also rose in the course of the period, but more important was the grandiose scale of royal ambition. Richard I's reign witnessed an extremely expensive struggle against the French monarchy, as well as the very costly crusading venture. The need to pay the king's ransom, after his capture while returning from the east, was a further financial blow. John's determination to recapture Normandy, lost in 1204, involved him not only in the costly expedition to Poitou in 1214, but also in a complex scheme of foreign alliances. His plans were echoed by those of Edward I in his French war of 1294–8, which involved English forces fighting in Gascony, while a royal expedition to Flanders was mounted with the support of a grand alliance of princes from the Low Countries, Germany and Burgundy. Edward's alliances cost him in the region of £150,000, though the obligations he had entered into amounted to much more than that. The total cost of his French war probably approached £750,000. War within the British Isles was not as expensive as continental warfare, but John spent lavishly on his Irish expedition of 1210, and Wales was a drain on royal resources at intervals throughout the thirteenth century. In Edward I's later years, involvement in Scotland proved expensive and unprofitable. Henry III was not a warlike king, but he was drawn into papal designs on Sicily and southern Italy. In return for the candidature of his second son Edmund to the Sicilian throne, he engaged to provide huge sums of money: in 1255 he agreed to pay the pope over £90,000 within eighteen months. There were other ways, too, in which the crown spent lavishly in the thirteenth century. Westminster Abbey still stands as a monument, among other things, to Henry III's extravagance, costing him at least £40,000, or roughly two years' ordinary revenue. Edward I's castles in North Wales cost the equivalent of a full-scale campaign, some £80,000.

The normal revenues of the crown were simply not sufficient to cope with such demands. It has been calculated that in the early 1240s, if taxation income is excluded, the king's total expendable income stood at around £33,000, and this was in a period when heavy financial pressure was placed on the Jews, and considerable efforts were being made to maximise income from such sources as the courts of law. An exchequer estimate of 1284, excluding what came in from the customs, put royal income at just under £19,000 a year.[2] There were many reasons why regular income was so inadequate. The stock of royal land, vast during the Conqueror's reign, had been very considerably depleted as a result of the needs of royal patronage. In addition, it proved impossible for the crown to do as private landlords did, and profit from the economic circumstances of the period by engaging in a system of direct management, rather than leasing out estates at rates which inflation rapidly made unprofitable. When attempts were made, in the late 1230s and in the late 1270s, the task of administering such widespread and extensive lands proved to be too great for a hard-pressed royal bureaucracy.

Taxation was the obvious solution to the dilemma. There were, of course, certain traditional rights that the king possessed. There were the traditional feudal aids. The right to demand military service from his tenants-in-chief might be commuted into a cash payment, known as scutage if it was based on the old assessments of knight service, or as a fine if calculated more arbitrarily. The royal demesnes were subject to an arbitrary tax, tallage. The Jews were regarded as royal property, and were therefore subject to royal levies at the king's whim. Even in the late twelfth century, however, such sources had not proved adequate. Under John, a tallage in 1210 probably raised some £10,000, but by the early fourteenth century, the level of receipts from a tallage was under £5,000. In 1254 a feudal aid on the occasion of the knighting of the king's son should have raised about £12,000, collected as it was as the rate of £2 a knight's fee, but it is most unlikely that such a sum was in fact collected. Even though he was fully entitled to an aid on the occasion of his daughter's marriage, Edward I negotiated it as a grant in 1290, but delayed collection until 1303. It probably yielded about £7,000. Far more effective than such taxes were levies of a non-feudal character, which were not limited as tallage was to the royal demesne, or as feudal aids were, to an assessment based on the knight's fee.

Under Richard I various types of taxes were collected, such as a carucage, or tax on plough-lands. What proved most effective was a tax on an assessment of the value of people's movable goods and rents. This was modelled on the taxes introduced by the church to pay for crusades, notably the Saladin Tithe of 1188. This was followed up in John's reign, when the most significant tax was that taken in 1207, consisting of payment of 1 s. for every mark of the assessed value of movables and rents, or approximately a thirteenth. This was decided upon at a council held early in the year at Oxford. In the writs authorising the tax it was claimed that consent had been provided by common counsel to this levy, and it was certainly the case that there had been considerable debate. The purpose of the tax was explained as being 'for the defence of the realm and the recovery of our rights'.[3] The levy was astonishingly successful, bringing in about £60,000.

Successful taxes are not popular among those who pay them. John's opponents were anxious to make it absolutely clear that the king had no arbitrary power to levy taxation of this character. It was inevitable that Magna Carta should tackle the question. Clause 12 stated that no scutage or aid should be levied, save by common counsel of the realm. The only exceptions were the three feudal aids to which the king was entitled. The clause was not wholly satisfactory. Scutage, properly speaking, was money payable in lieu of military service, but as consent was not required for the summons of the feudal host, it was hardly logical to demand consent for scutage. In fact, the term was probably not intended in its technical sense. John had levied frequent scutages, and in clause 12 the word probably simply meant tax in a broad way. Aid was equally imprecise, but the tax of 1207 was surely in the minds of those who drafted the Charter. Clause 14 proceeded to deal with the question of how the common counsel of the realm was to be obtained. The great men – prelates, earls and major barons – were to be summoned individually, while sheriffs and bailiffs were responsible for asking the other tenants-in-chief to attend. The assembly was defined in purely feudal terms. Only those who held land directly from the crown were to be summoned.[4]

Clause 12 of Magna Carta 1215 was not included in the reissues, and did not therefore become part of English law. Nevertheless, the idea that the king should obtain consent for such extraordinary taxes as the levies on movables could hardly be abandoned. It may be that it was the inclusion of scutage that made the clause unacceptable, rather than the demand that consent should be obtained. Even John had claimed consent for the thirteenth of 1207, however much his subjects may have doubted the reality of that consent. In 1220 a carucage was collected, and the writs claimed that consent had been given by all the magnates and faithful subjects. By 1232, when a tax of a fortieth was levied, the government was claiming that it had the consent of all from archbishops, through earls and barons, right down to villeins, though how the latter can possibly have been consulted defeats the imagination. In 1237 a more realistic formula stated that the magnates and knights had consented for themselves and their villeins.[5]

Contemporaries were not very clear about the precise nature of the consent that was provided in the years up to 1237, and the situation is confusing for historians. There was a view that consent was an individual matter. When the bishop of Winchester, Peter des Roches, was charged with 159 marks as his share of the aid of 1217, which was collected on the basis of the number of knight's fees held, he declared that he had not given his consent to the tax, and that he should not have to pay. His argument was accepted by the council. Some magnates refused to allow the collection of the tax of 1232 on their lands for several years, on the same grounds that they had not given their individual consent to it.[6] At the same time, the phraseology of royal writs can be taken to imply communal, corporate consent provided by the magnates present at the great councils. Individual objections should not be allowed to override what had been generally agreed. It is hard to see how an assembly of the type defined in Magna Carta clause 14 could provide such national assent, for there was no system of representation, but the magnates considered it appropriate that they should speak on behalf of the realm as a whole. The government obviously found it politic to claim that general assent had indeed been given.

Arguments derived from Roman law provide a different dimension to the problems of taxation. In theory, according to the doctrines of Roman law, if a state of urgent necessity could be shown to exist, then a prince had a right to obtain taxes from his subjects. Consent, according to this theory, had to be freely given, but could not be refused.[7] This theory of necessity was employed in the thirteenth century period by the papacy in its requests for funds for the crusade, and Henry III's government certainly used similar vocabulary. The carucage of 1220 was 'for our great necessity, the urgent pressure of our debts and the preservation of our land of Poitou'. In 1254 knights were summoned to discuss what sort of aid should be granted 'in such necessity' as the situation in Gascony created.[8]

It is quite clear, however, that taxes were not in practice conceded with the ease which might have been expected, had the doctrine of necessity been widely accepted. Two meetings were needed before the grant of 1225 was conceded: three before that of 1232. There was great difficulty in negotiating that of 1237, and thereafter Henry III was unable to obtain grants of further taxes on movables until the very end of his reign. One way this can be explained is by arguing that the doctrine had the effect of shifting the grounds on which a tax might be refused. If consent could not be rejected outright, it might still be possible to deny that any necessity existed. There might be arguments that the king's debts did not constitute a national necessity, and that threats to his lands in France were no concern of his English subjects. In 1254 it was argued, with ample justification as events turned out, that there was no threat from Castile against Gascony, despite what the king claimed. G. L. Harriss has shown that the English barons took up different positions when feudal aids or feudal service were demanded, and when the question was one of national taxation assessed on a valuation of movable goods. The magnates, in his view, were prepared to do all they could to perform their feudal obligations, while refusing to grant aids on behalf of the realm as a whole, on the grounds that no national necessity existed. A campaign in Gascony might be the king's war, but might not be a national necessity for his English realm.[9]

It is not clear that the magnates really interpreted the king's demands for taxation in the sophisticated terms of Roman law. Churchmen certainly had the intellectual training to do so, but laymen are less likely to have been conversant with the ideas of the schools. Nor is it even easy to be certain that the king's use of the language of necessity amounted to a formal statement that he considered that a state of necessity existed, in the technical sense demanded by Roman law. The terminology may have amounted to nothing more than a factual statement of the position in which the king found himself, with no deeper implications. Harriss argues that had a real right of refusal been established, then it would have been used in the period 1294–7, when taxes were levied annually. That is to make a considerable chronological jump across the years between 1237 and 1269. There is every indication that the magnates exercised a real right to consent in Henry III's reign, rather than simply debating the issue of whether or not a genuine necessity existed.

Examination of the circumstances in which one particular grant was made may help to elucidate the situation as it was in the early part of Henry III's reign. In 1237 the magnates met in January to consider the king's request for a tax. The demand was put by William Raleigh, probably the ablest of the king's councillors. He explained that the money was needed, partly because of the incompetence of former royal officials, and partly in order to pay the expenses of the king's marriage, and the cost of his sister's dowry. He promised that the money raised in taxation would be kept for the necessary requirements of the realm, and offered the possibility that the magnates might elect representatives to control the way in which it was spent. After discussions, far greater concessions than these were obtained in return for the grant. Magna Carta was confirmed once more, and increased security was given to men who held royal demesne manors by charter. The process of recovering royal lands which had been granted out was cut back sharply. Three magnates were added to the king's council. Limitations were imposed on royal exploitation of forest rights, and measures were taken to prevent abuse of the royal right of prise, the compulsory purchase of wine and foodstuffs. It was decided that assessment of the tax should be delayed until September. With the harvest just in, the tax would be more profitable that way, but it may also be that the magnates wished for a delay, so that they could test the king's intentions to fulfil his promises of concessions. The greatest concession of all was that Henry III had to promise that he would not collect any more taxes of this type.

Matthew Paris's account of the meeting in January – which one official source terms, for the first time, a parliament – makes it clear that individual summonses had been issued to the magnates, as Magna Carta had required, but the purpose of the assembly had not been explained in them. Raleigh's speech did not use the language of necessity, save in the promise of how the money raised would be spent. The objections of the magnates, according to Paris, were that frequent taxes had been levied in the past, but that the king had never driven any of his enemies from the land, or extended the boundaries of the realm, but that rather, he had subjected native-born Englishmen to aliens. This could be read as an argument that past claims of necessity had not proved to be justified, or as a straightforward exposition of the situation as the magnates saw it. The discussions were clearly extremely difficult and tense: there was no ready acknowledgement of any obligation by the magnates.[10]

It does not appear that the magnates actually rejected any royal demands for grants of taxation until 1242. When Henry III asked for aid for his coming expedition to Poitou in that year, he met with determined resistance. In an attempt to break the collective will, the king summoned individual magnates to private interviews, but without success. He had to turn to feudal methods of taxation, to heavy taxation of the Jews, and to attempts to exploit the traditional revenues of the crown. A further attempt to negotiate an aid in 1244–5 was unsuccessful. The magnates adopted an electoral system to choose twelve of their number, both lay and ecclesiastical, to act on behalf of the community. Complaints were made that the king had not kept Magna Carta as he had promised, and that previous taxes had not been spent to the profit of king and kingdom. The so-called Paper Constitution was drawn up, which included a requirement that all money granted should be spent for the benefit of the king and the realm, under the supervision of four 'conservators of liberties'. Henry was not prepared to make any concessions, and in place of a tax on movables, eventual agreement was reached in 1245 that the king should be granted a feudal aid for the marriage of his eldest daughter, to be taken at the far from generous rate of 20 s. on each knight's fee. This, of course, was a tax that the king was perfectly entitled to take, but the rate was perhaps open for negotiation, as was the question of how many fees were subject to taxation.[11] In 1254 the only lay tax that the king could obtain was a feudal aid for the knighting of his son Edward, taken at the rate of three marks on each knight's fee, an aid to which he had a formal right. The negotiations in that year were very significant, for knights of the shire were summoned by the regency government operating in the king's absence in Gascony to discuss the question of taxation. This was done because it was considered that the magnates were contributing to the king's efforts in Gascony in a different way, by providing military service. Whether or not the representatives made any substantial contribution to the decision that was taken to resist the crown's requests is not known: it seems unlikely. An important precedent had nevertheless been set for consultation with the shires. Henry asked for a grant again in 1257, but was rebuffed. In 1258 he once more requested an aid, but the magnates were horrified at the scale of the debts he had incurred as a result of the candidature of his son Edmund for the Sicilian throne, and not surprisingly rejected the royal request.

This period from 1237 was remarkable, with consistent refusals to grant taxes. This led to greater burdens being laid on the populace in other ways, particularly as the king's financial situation became more desperate in the 1250s. The sheriffs had a greater financial obligation placed on them, and considerable efforts were made to raise as much money as possible from such sources as the Jews, and to increase the profitability of justice to the king. All this pressure contributed to the general discontent which was an important part of the background to the crisis of 1258.

Taxation was not, of course, purely a matter for the laity, but it did not prove easy in this period to negotiate taxes with the clergy. John failed to obtain a grant from them in 1207, but the opportunities provided by the interdict enabled him to profit in other ways from the wealth of the church. Under Henry III the church began to pay substantial taxes to the papacy, and some of the proceeds of these came to the crown. Direct negotiations also took place. The tax of a fifteenth in 1225 was not levied on the beneficed clergy, and after much debate, a clerical tax of a sixteenth was agreed in the following year. This did not take the same form as the lay taxes, but was based on the valuations for a crusading tax imposed in 1216. Thereafter the clergy proved obdurate in refusing grants of taxation, though eventually, after long discussions in parliament in 1253, it was agreed that Henry could have the receipts of a tenth for three years. This was based on a new assessment, and in 1254 the pope extended the period of the tax from three to five years. Although it was, in theory, a crusading tax, it was papal policy to use the proceeds for the Sicilian adventure, and in 1255 the king's vow to go on crusade was converted into one to go to Sicily. Henry could not collect the two additional years tax, granted to him by the pope, without further authority, and so in 1257 the matter was discussed at a meeting in Westminster. Negotiations were not easy: the prelates insisted on a delay so that they could consult the clergy at large, but eventually an offer of £52,000 was made to the king.[12]

Henry's problems in negotiating a tax certainly contributed to the start of the crisis of 1258, but questions of taxation did not figure largely in the complex political events of the succeeding years. Circumstances were such that it was not possible for Henry to obtain grants, though a tallage was raised in 1260. In 1264, after the king's defeat at the battle of Lewes, the prelates granted a tenth for one year, providing striking evidence of the support that Simon de Montfort's regime received from the church.[13]

At the end of Henry's reign, after the king's recovery of power in 1265, the clergy were taxed under papal auspices, with much of the proceeds going to the crown. Then, in 1268, negotiations began for a new tax to be paid by the laity, in order to pay for the crusade which Henry III himself initially intended to go on, but which his son Edward led in his place. The discussions were lengthy, extending over several parliaments. The most significant aspect of them was the involvement of knights and burgesses: at the October parliament of 1269 both groups were almost certainly present in parliament, along with representatives of the lower clergy. It was no easy task to set up a tax on movables after such a long intermission: there was a curious process by which county representatives apparently elected baronial assessors. The rate of the tax which was finally agreed was a twentieth, which raised some £30,000.[14]

Under Edward I taxation became much more regular than it had been under Henry III, and the importance of the taxes on movables, and on clerical incomes, as against other forms of tax, became still clearer. There were nine taxes on movables in the course of the reign, with assessments ranging from over £116,000 to under £35,000. Four of the taxes were collected at a double rate, such as the tenth and sixth of 1294: the higher rate was paid by the towns and ancient demesne, as an alternative to having a tallage imposed on them. The purpose of the majority of the taxes was, of course, to pay for war, but they did not all fit conveniently into the theory of necessity. That of 1275 was intended to pay off the huge debts which Edward had incurred on his crusade, while that of 1290, the most successful of all the taxes of the reign, was needed to pay for the costs of the king's recent stay in Gascony, and the expenses of his efforts to obtain the release of Charles of Salerno from custody in Aragon. The concessions Edward made in return for this tax were considerable. The aggressive *Quo Warranto* campaign of investigation into the jurisdictional rights held by the magnates was tempered by compromise. Above all, the king exiled all the Jews from the land. This was a popular move, and although Edward was depriving himself of what had once been a lucrative financial resource, the Jews were no longer wealthy, after so many years of royal levies. Any calculation would show that the tax of a fifteenth was worth much more than the Jews could have provided over very many years.

The lay taxes were not all granted in the same way, but Edward's reign did see the principle firmly established that representatives should give their consent. The parliament of 1275 was probably one of the best attended of the medieval period, for it had an unusually large number of burgesses present. In 1283 the tax of a thirtieth had, at least in part, the character of being an alternative to active military service: the tax was not conceded in parliament, but in two regional assemblies, to which shire representatives were summoned. In 1290 the final go-ahead for the tax was given when knights of the shire were asked to attend at Westminster, to consent to what had already been discussed by the magnates. Knights of the shire were involved in granting the taxes of 1294, 1295 and 1296.

Taxation was a major issue in 1297. There was the question, already discussed, of the clerical refusal to pay taxes, because of the papal prohibition in the bull *Clericis Laicos*. In addition, there was what was seen as an attempt to impose, rather than negotiate, a lay tax. The king was under very considerable financial pressure, and instead of consulting a full parliament, held an informal gathering, sardonically described by one chronicler as consisting simply of people standing round in the royal chamber. No formally summoned representatives were present. In August of that year the two leading lay opponents of the king, the earls of Norfolk and Hereford, appeared at the exchequer, with their armed retainers, and prevented the tax from going ahead. When there was a genuine national emergency in the autumn, following the defeat of the English forces at Stirling Bridge in Scotland, there was no question of reviving this eighth: instead, an entirely new grant of a ninth was made, with the participation of representatives.

Edward's attempt to impose a tax of an eighth in the summer of 1297 was seen by his opponents as reducing them to the level of unfree villeins, subject to arbitrary exactions by their lord. It was unacceptable that the king should behave like this, and the question of how taxes should be granted was dealt with in the resolution of the crisis of 1297. The baronial draft document, known as *De Tallagio*, demanded that consent be given by archbishops, bishops and other prelates, earls, barons, knights, burgesses and other free men of the realm. This document was not acceptable to the government: in the text which was agreed, the *Confirmatio Cartarum*, the vaguer statement that taxation should be taken 'by the common assent of the realm' was employed. Neither document, interestingly, included any mention of parliament as the place where consent should be obtained. As usual, the arguments that took place in 1297 can be interpreted in various ways, but as far as the king was concerned, his case was put in simple terms, of the allegiance owed to a lord by his subjects. The technical language of necessity was not employed, as Edward stressed the fact that he was risking life and limb on behalf of his people, and the least that they could do was to pay him taxes.[15]

Arguments over taxation continued after 1297. In 1298 the king told the clergy that he intended to finance his Scottish war from his own resources, 'of his own', but in view of the heavy costs involved this was not practicable.[16] In 1300 there were difficult negotiations in parliament, and although a twentieth was agreed, the king decided not to take the tax, so much did he resent the conditions imposed on him in return for it. In the next year, 1301, matters were more difficult still, and Edward accepted a fifteenth, primarily in return for clear assurances that he would accept the verdict of a full investigation of the forest boundaries, which he had been resisting ever since 1298. It is also likely that, like his father in 1237, he promised to take no more taxes on movables. Such a promise was unlikely to be kept, but the next tax, that of 1306, did have a rather different character, in that it was negotiated as an alternative to a feudal aid to which the king was perfectly entitled, on the occasion of the knighting of his eldest son. Curiously, although representatives of the shires were present at the meeting when the tax

was granted, the writs summoning them had not demanded
that they be in possession of full powers to act on behalf of
their local community, as was normal.[17]

The role of the representatives in granting taxes is enig-
matic. There is no account of events in parliament to reveal
what actually happened, and there is very little to suggest
that they did anything more than give a passive consent to
what was decided by their social superiors. One chronicle
account states that in 1294 it was the earl of Gloucester who
was responsible for arguing that the rate of a third, suggested by the government, was excessive, and that a tenth
and sixth was agreed as a result. There is no indication of an
initiative taken by any knights of the shire, with the sole
exception of the bill presented in parliament in 1301 by
Henry Keighley. Yet if the representatives did so little, why
were they summoned with such regularity? It could well be
that it was realised that if taxes were negotiated simply with
the magnates, then there might be considerable popular
hostility to them: it would be wrong to assume that the
populace as a whole was completely politically illiterate. Yet
there is no evidence of any such feelings. The magnates
obviously felt a certain reluctance to make grants in isolation,
for when they agreed in 1290 that the king could collect an
aid on the occasion of his daughter's marriage, they made it
clear that they did so 'for themselves and the community of
the realm, as far as they could'.[18]

The proviso indicates an uneasiness not possessed by the
magnates earlier in the thirteenth century, a feeling that they
alone did not constitute the community. Such attitudes,
along with a realisation that taxes of a national character did
require a truly national consent, do more perhaps to explain
the type of consent given to taxation under Edward I than
any assertiveness on the part of the knightly classes. It was,
too, obviously considered right that those who were to pay
should give their consent. In 1275 the king had summoned
very large numbers of urban representatives to parliament,
because they were required to give their agreement to the
imposition of new customs duties, levied primarily on

exports of wool. The merchants would pay this tax: therefore the merchants should be asked for their consent.

The political importance of the power of the community of the realm to grant taxation was well demonstrated in Edward I's later years. It is not surprising that this financial weapon also proved potent in the first major crisis of Edward II's reign, that of the Ordinances of 1311, a crisis which in many ways can be seen as the conclusion of the arguments which had begun in 1297. In 1307 Edward had been granted a tax of a twentieth for the war in Scotland, and in 1309 one of a twenty-fifth, for which the king had to make concessions regarding prises and other matters. The opposition suspended collection of this tax as a means of forcing Edward to agree to the appointment of Ordainers in 1310. The Ordinances took time to draft, and were finally issued in the autumn of 1311.

Financial matters had an important place in the Ordinances. It was laid down that the revenues of the land should all be paid directly to the exchequer: substantial resources had previously been channelled directly to the household department of the wardrobe. The new customs duties introduced in 1303 were abolished. Prises should be paid for, and the king should live of his own. Taxation on movables, however, did not feature. This was not because it was unimportant, but because sufficient safeguards already existed. These taxes could only be taken with proper assent by the community of the realm, and that assent was normally provided in parliament.

It was one thing to control the grant of taxation, and quite another to influence the way in which the money was spent. Here, there was less success in controlling the crown. The more taxation became a regular element in royal revenue, the harder it was to ensure that the money went where it was intended. In 1225 the bishops of Bath and Salisbury were appointed to act as receivers and custodians of the tax of a fifteenth, and they ensured that the bulk of the money was spent on Richard of Cornwall's expedition to Gascony. In 1237 a condition of the grant of a fortieth was that it should be spent on necessary purposes. This, in the opinion of the magnates, was not done, and this was given as one reason for rejecting the king's request for a further tax in 1242. Taxes, however, were separately administered and accounted for until as late as 1290. Only then was taxation revenue incorporated into the normal receipts of the crown. It became more difficult to know how the money that had been collected was spent. The *Confirmatio Cartarum* of 1297 stated that taxes should be spent on the common profit of the realm, but no effective mechanism was set up to ensure that this was done.[19]

Indirect taxation was not the subject of as much argument as the taxes on movable goods. In part this was because by their nature, customs duties had a more permanent character than other taxes, and were not therefore subject to frequent renegotiation. King John, as in so many ways setting precedents for the future, levied duties on imports and exports for a brief period, but it was not until 1275 that a regular customs system was introduced, following a short-term precedent established in 1266. It was agreed in parliament in 1275 that 6 *s.* 8 *d.* should be levied on every sack of wool exported from the realm. The scheme was probably suggested by an Italian merchant, and the duties were intended to provide a convenient means of repaying the Italians for their loans. Receipts fluctuated around a level of £10,000 a year. Then, in 1294, under the pressure of war, the king turned to trade as a means of raising additional funds. There was even a suggestion that a sales tax should be introduced. Initially, it was decided that there should be a compulsory seizure of all the wool in the land – a kind of nationalisation – which the crown would then export at a considerable profit. The merchants objected, and instead of the seizure, additional customs duties of £2 a sack were imposed. This was done without full approval being obtained in parliament, and in 1297 this *maltolt*, as it was termed, was the subject of vehement protests. The burden of the tax on the country was stressed more than the breach of constitutional proprieties. During its brief period of existence, from

1294 to 1297, this additional £2 duty raised about £116,000. In 1303 the king negotiated another additional customs duty. Initial soundings among English merchants were favourable but, when a meeting was held, they refused to make a grant. The foreign merchants, on the other hand, agreed to pay an extra 3 s. 4 d. on each sack of wool exported, as well as duties on other goods. In return, they received significant freedom to trade as they wished in England. In 1311 this New Custom, as it was known, was abolished in the Ordinances. It was not a heavy burden for the country to bear, and a system which charged alien merchants more than their English counterparts might appear attractive. The grant, however, had not had general approval, and was clearly unconstitutional. There were also considerable objections to the *Carta mercatoria*, the charter of privileges which Edward I had issued to the foreign merchants. It would not, however, be until the 1360s that the commons in parliament obtained full control over grants of customs revenue.[20]

It is not easy to determine to what extent deep-felt constitutional principles were merged with a straightforward resentment at the financial burdens involved in taxation. In the fourteenth century a bitter poet commented that it was nothing for great men to grant taxes, as it was the poor who had to pay.[21] Although the poorest were exempt from taxation, surviving assessment records show that the burden of payment extended deep into society. It is, however, impossible to determine the implications for Osbert, who lived in Kirby in Lincolnshire, of paying 5 s. 4 d. as his contribution to the fifteenth of 1225, when he possessed ten cattle, forty sheep, one pig, a one-eyed horse and a quantity of grain.[22] The tax burden on an individual magnate was undoubtedly proportionately lower than on men such as Osbert. There is no doubt that at some periods, notably the 1290s, the weight of taxation was considerable for all. It might amount to 25 per cent or more of the budget of a religious house facing the combined weight of lay and ecclesiastical taxes. It is striking that the estate book of a Northamptonshire knight, Henry de Bray, shows that he was not investing on any scale in improvements to his property during the years of heavy taxation: he celebrated the end of wartime austerity by building a water-mill at a cost of almost £10. During the period when the additional customs duty of 40 s. a sack was in force, the average price in England obtained by woolgrowers fell by about £1 a sack, some 15 or 20 per cent. This would have affected both great and small, cutting back incomes at a time when bad harvests were driving prices upwards. A genuine concern at the scale of the burden of taxation emerges from the anti-royal propaganda of 1297.[23]

The power to control the levy of taxation was a potent political weapon. The thirteenth century marks the beginning of a long history of concessions being won from the government in return for much needed financial supply. The development of a system of corporate national consent in parliament ranks as an achievement of the greatest significance for the future. Historians are not unanimous in their interpretations of the situation in the thirteenth century. For those who consider that ideas drawn from Roman law were of fundamental importance, stress is placed on the question of necessity. The area for negotiation between the ruler and subjects, in these terms, was a limited one, with the latter having no real power to reject royal demands save in cases where no necessity could be demonstrated. While such concepts were of undeniable importance as far as the church was concerned, it is hard to accept that laymen would have found them persuasive. Under John, the scale of royal taxation was an important part of the background to the crisis of 1215 and Magna Carta. In the next reign, bargaining over taxation was central to the political process until 1237. Thereafter no grants of taxes on movables could be obtained until 1269. Taxation did not, therefore, loom large as an issue in the period 1258–65, though the pressures on both government and country that resulted from the king's financial difficulties were major factors leading to the crises of those years. In Edward I's reign, the crown became increasingly dependent on taxes which could be collected only after a proper grant had been made by magnates and representatives. When, under extreme pressure, the king attempted to impose a tax in 1298, he was firmly rebuffed. In 1300 and 1301 a pattern was emerging of taxes being granted in return for redress of grievances, and by 1311 it was apparent that withholding taxation was a most effective political weapon in the hands of the community of the realm.

8

PARLIAMENT AND COMMUNITY

THE LANGUAGE of community became fashionable in the thirteenth century. Magna Carta referred to 'the community of the whole land'. In the 1240s *universitas*, a term effectively synonymous with 'community', was the favoured expression. The Provisions of Oxford of 1258 included an oath to be sworn by the community of England (*le commun de Engleterre*). Simon de Montfort's parliament of 1265 was summoned to discuss matters affecting the community of the realm. The *Confirmatio Cartarum* of 1297 referred to both the community of the land, and of the realm. What precisely was meant by such phrases is often not easy to determine. The community might appear as a threat to the crown, as in 1215, or as consenting to royal legislation, as in 1275 in the first statute of Westminster. Parliament was another fashionable word. Historians have struggled to find an exact definition for a term which often lacked true precision. It began to be applied to certain royal councils from the 1230s. By 1311, when the Ordinances were issued, consent was to be provided in parliament, and no mention was made of the community. The transformations that took place in the course of the thirteenth century were not merely matters of verbal definition: they were fundamental shifts in the political structure. They present historians with thorny problems.

The idea of a community taking political action had radical overtones. Twice in the twelfth century, during the Anarchy of Stephen's reign and in the course of Richard I's absence on crusade, the citizens of London formed a sworn commune. They were, no doubt, influenced by the communal movement on the continent: in Italy and the Low Countries the urban commune was the instrument by which towns and cities gained independence from external rule. Whether that was a precedent in the mind of the men who drafted the Articles of the Barons and Magna Carta in 1215 must be doubtful. It was laid down that should the king fail to do justice, he might be distrained by the twenty-five barons 'with the community of the whole land'. No trumpeting accompanied the use of this phrase, and there was no attempt to define what was meant. One chronicler had described the coastal defence scheme of 1205 as a 'commune', perhaps because it involved oaths sworn by all those who were to bear arms in defence of the country, but it would be far-fetched to see in this reference any precedent for the usage adopted in Magna Carta. In the royal writ about the scheme, King John referred to the consent he had obtained from archbishops, bishops, earls, barons and all his loyal subjects, but on other occasions reference was made to 'common counsel and assent'.[1] It was perhaps not a very large step to move from that to the idea of the community of the land. It would be wrong, in any case, to make too much of the phraseology adopted in 1215 in Magna Carta, for it found few echoes for some years.

When the writs ordering collection of the taxes of 1232 and 1237 were issued, they specified in great if less than convincing detail which groups had provided consent. There was no use of phraseology which implied the consent of the community as a whole.[2] However, the idea of common counsel was stressed when Henry III tried to dismiss the chancellor, Ralph Neville in 1236. Neville refused to hand over the great seal. He claimed that he had received it by common counsel of the realm, and could not surrender it without common assent. Matthew Paris's account, however, makes no mention of the community of the land as providing such common assent.[3]

There was a change of emphasis in 1244. The Paper Constitution, almost certainly drawn up in that year, included a scheme for the election of four men 'by common assent'. They were to be responsible for meetings of the *universitas*, the community. In 1245 a letter of complaint was sent to the General Council at Lyons held by Innocent IV, by the 'barons, knights, and the *universitas* of the baronage of England'. In the next year two clerks went to Rome as emissaries of the *universitas* of England. There was evidently a concept of a baronial community, and this found further political expression in 1249 when, according to Matthew Paris, a tournament was held at Brackley between 'many of the knights of the *universitas*, who wished to be known as bachelors', and the aliens.[4]

In 1258 the concept of the community of the land was expressed in a new and forceful way. The Provisions of Oxford set out the oath to be sworn by the *commune*. There are dangers in translating the contemporary terminology as 'community'. The French term used was *commune*, the Latin *communitas*, and 'commune' is perhaps closer in meaning than is 'community', though both terms have unacceptable present-day overtones. Interpretations inevitably differ. For Treharne, there was no doubt that the community in question was the community of the king's tenants-in-chief. More recently, Clanchy has offered a persuasive interpretation, which stresses the identity of 'community' with the notion of a sworn commune. At the outset of the crisis, on 12 April, a group of seven influential magnates, including Simon de Montfort and the earl of Gloucester, swore to support each other in terms which anticipated the oath of the *commune* of the Oxford provisions. This was surely the germ of the *commune* of England: a small, powerful group to which other barons swiftly attached themselves. A recent parallel was provided by the Commune of Acre, a sworn baronial confederacy in the Kingdom of Jerusalem, bitterly opposed to the emperor Frederick II's claim to rule there.[5]

The Provisions of Oxford set out the details of the oath sworn by the *commune* of England, essentially a promise to assist one another, and to take nothing unjustly. The document also lists the twelve men, chosen by the barons, who were to represent the *commune* at the three annual parliaments that were to be held. The *commune* agreed to accept what was done by the twelve on their behalf, and it was stated that this was in order to spare its expenses. Where tax grants were concerned, the *commune* was to be represented by twenty-four. This *commune* was surely no more than a limited sworn baronial confederacy, and its nature explains the otherwise puzzlingly low level of representation envisaged.

The *commune* of 1258 soon developed into the community in a much wider sense. This is suggested by a letter describing events after the parliament stating that the Lusignans were opposed to the Provisions and the community of the realm. They had fled 'like traitors to the lord king and the community'. When a royal clerk translated the term *commune de nostre reaume* into English, he rendered it as 'the native people of our kingdom' (londes folk on ure kuneriche). The final clause of the Provisions of Westminster of 1259 declared that the measures had been made 'by the king and his council and the twelve elected by the common counsel [*par le commun conseil*], in the presence of the community of England'.[6] The language of community began to be widely used. In 1259 there was the incident of the protest of a body calling itself the 'Community of the Bachelors of England', a phrase curiously reminiscent of the Brackley tournament of 1249. Just who the 'bachelors' were is a question which has been much debated, and which can never be determined: they were clearly a sworn group of those irritated at the slow progress of reform, but whether they were of baronial or knightly rank is not apparent. By 1264 the term *commune* was being applied lower in the social spectrum: a chronicler could speak of the rejection of St Louis's arbitration between king and barons by 'almost the whole *commune* of the middling people of England'.[7]

The idea of the community of the realm was central to the baronial reform movement under Simon de Montfort. The *Song of Lewes* explained that the king should be advised by the community, and that note should be taken of the opinions of the *universitas*, who best knew the laws that governed them. It was a matter of concern to the community that appropriate councillors should provide advice for the king. In a theoretical examination of the political structure, the author stated that 'we place in the forefront the *universitas*'. The wording of the *Forma Regiminis* is intriguing. It provides for the replacement of any of the three electors 'if it shall seem necessary to the community of the prelates and barons', but also states that the ordinance as a whole received the consent 'of the prelates, barons and also of the community as that time present'. There is a danger of reading too much into such phrases, though the implication is that the prelates and barons by themselves formed a community, but that the community of the realm was much more extensive. This fits with the fact that in the summonses to parliament issued early in 1265, the language of community was not used in the writs sent to the bishops and magnates, but did appear in some summonses to the men of the Cinque Ports and the counties. By the close of the period of baronial reform and rebellion, it is apparent that ideas about the community had reached deep into English society. The men of Peatling Magna, a Leicestershire village, could accuse a group of royalists of 'going against the community of the realm and against the barons'.[8] There is no clear definition of what men meant by the community at this time. Certainly the *commune* of 1258 can be interpreted as being a narrow baronial body, but there was also a much broader concept at work, of the community as a whole, extending beyond the bounds of the baronage.

According to the Provisions of Oxford, it was in parliament that the community were to be represented three times a year. The nature of parliament in this period has been the subject of much controversy. For Richardson and Sayles, who have argued their case repeatedly, without recruiting many followers, parliament was above all a court. The activity of the king and his council hearing petitions and determining cases was the essential core of parliament. If great affairs of state happen to be discussed in parliament, that had no great relevance, for such matters could have been discussed in great councils just as much as parliaments.[9] Other historians, perhaps less concerned with establishing precise definitions, have stressed the wide range of business, political, financial and legislative, which took place in parliaments. The role of parliament in the grant of taxation, for instance, is often stressed. Parliament can be seen as the institution where the community of the realm found its voice.

There is certainly a strong case for regarding parliament in purely legal terms. The term itself was first used in an official government record in 1236, when a case was postponed to be heard in parliament when it met early in the following year. In the Ordinances of 1311 it was stated that parliament ought to be held at least once a year, and twice if necessary. This was specifically to ensure that cases were not unnecessarily delayed. As the great legal historian Maitland pointed out, when he edited the parliamentary records of 1305, parliament remained in session after the magnates and representatives had departed, and consisted of no more than the king's council and those who brought cases before it.[10] If the intention of the historian is to find the irreducible minimum that could be regarded as a parliament, then this will be the correct interpretation. Taxes were not granted in every parliament, and indeed some taxes were granted in assemblies that were not called parliaments. Representatives were not summoned to all parliaments: far from it. Important questions such as those of war and peace might be discussed in parliaments, but they might also be discussed in other royal councils, such as that held at Devizes in 1282 when it was decided to campaign against the rebellious Welsh. It is surely a mistake to try to interpret the parliaments of this period in terms of what the assembly developed into in more modern periods. Yet a narrow legal definition of parliament misses much. To try to reduce parliament to its barest minimum is to adopt a misleading approach which fails to reveal the true nature of the assembly. If its role is to be understood, it is necessary to take into account the full

range of activities that took place in parliament, irrespective
of whether or not they were exclusive to parliament.

In the period leading up to the crisis of 1258, it does not
appear that royal clerks adopted any careful definition:
assemblies were more often termed colloquiums than parliaments. It was not until ten years after the first appearance of
the word parliament in an official record that the chronicler
Matthew Paris first employed it. In the parliaments of this
period, the various different courts of exchequer, king's
bench and common pleas would be present, under the
overriding authority of the king and his great council. Major
events, such as the trial of Simon de Montfort in 1252, when
charges were brought against him by the Gascons who had
suffered from his authoritarian rule in the duchy, took place
in parliament, but in addition a good many relatively minor
matters concerning individuals were also determined. Those
who attended parliaments were the king's ministers and
officials, and such members of the baronage who chose to
answer the king's summonses. It was becoming customary to
hold these parliaments at the dates of session of the law
courts. There was no sense among contemporaries that a
new institution had suddenly appeared. For a royal official
writing in 1244, the meeting at Runnymede when Magna
Carta was sealed had been a parliament.[11]

It would be very wrong to think that because the institution
of parliament was in its infancy, its meetings lacked importance. There are, unfortunately, no lists of those who were
summoned or of those who attended, but it is abundantly
clear that the parliaments of the 1240s and 1250s were great
occasions, at which most of the influential men of the
kingdom were present, and at which the major issues of the
day were discussed. Matthew Paris described the Easter
parliament of 1255, when so great a number had never
before been seen gathered together. Discussions centred on
the king's financial needs, and his failure to adhere to the
terms of Magna Carta. Election of a justiciar, and of the
chancellor and treasurer, by common counsel was demanded, but a confidant of the king let it be known that there was

no way that the king would agree to such a request. After much discussion it was agreed to continue debate at a further parliament in the autumn.[12] Such parliaments were major political occasions, and to emphasise above all the legal business at the expense of all the other activities yields a caricature rather than a portrait of the institution.

If 1258 suddenly saw the concept of the community of the realm acquire a new political significance, so too was this a vital year for parliament. That parliaments would be held regularly was assumed as a matter of course in the Provisions of Oxford, but clear guidelines were set out for the first time. There were to be three parliaments a year, at which the king's council would negotiate with the representatives of the *commune*. The precise dates of the meetings were set, and it was explained that the king's councillors were obliged to attend, whether or not they received summonses. The business was to consist of a review of the state of the realm, and 'the common business of the realm and of the king together'. It is apparent that these parliaments were to be more than sessions of a court: all the most important affairs of state were to be brought before parliament. None of this was of the king's choosing, and it is no surprise that the Oxford scheme did not last. Nothing more is heard of the twelve who represented the *commune* after the spring of 1261. Henry III succeeded in establishing the principle that parliament could not meet without the king. 'We inform you', he wrote early in 1260, 'that it is not our will that any parliament should be held in our realm while we are absent, since this is improper, and we do not believe it to be consonant with our honour'. In 1261 there was a ludicrous situation with a parliament summoned by the earls of Leicester and Gloucester, and a simultaneous summons to a royal parliament.[13] Henry, by stressing the royal character of parliament, had some success in neutralising the weapon that had been created in 1258. There was no question, however, of the king abandoning the holding of parliaments. Both the king and his opponents needed parliaments, and the revolutions that followed the battles of Lewes and Evesham in 1264 and 1265 caused no hiatus in the regular succession of parliaments. It was in parliament at Winchester in September 1265 that the task of restoring royal government was begun, and the next few years were to see parliaments held even more frequently than the three times a year demanded by the reformers of 1258.

Edward I learnt much from the reform movement, with which he had briefly been associated in 1259–60. It is no surprise that the concept of the community of the realm, which had become so clearly identified with Henry III's opponents, should have been harnessed by Edward when he became king.

In 1275 Edward held his first general parliament (to use the contemporary phrase) at Westminster. At it, the first Statute of Westminster was promulgated. The preamble declared that 'These are the establishments of King Edward ... made at Westminster ... by his council and by the assent of archbishops, bishops, abbots, priors, earls, barons and the community of the land summoned there'. The terminology echoed, and modified, that which had been used in the Provisions of Westminster of 1259. When the grant of customs duties was made in this parliament, it was said by the earl of Pembroke to have been made by the prelates, 'and earls, barons, and ourselves and the communities of the realm, at the instance and request of the merchants'.[14] In 1297, however, the earls opposing the king had no hesitation in claiming to speak on behalf of the community. There was an interesting difference in terminology. Edward's opponents described themselves in the Remonstrances presented in July 1297 as 'archbishops, bishops, earls, barons and all the community of the land', and the document continued with details of the grievances of 'the community'. However, when it came to a text produced by the crown, the *Confirmatio Cartarum*, drawn up in October, one clause referred to 'the community of the realm'.[15] The change from 'land' to 'realm' may not seem a large one, but it brought the community firmly within the orbit of the crown, where it had been outside it.

It would be wrong to lay too much stress on the use of the language of community by Edward I, for it was not used on every possible occasion. When, for example, he was justifying his declaration of war upon the Scots, he told the pope that he acted 'according to the laws and customs of our realm, and by the counsel of our nobles and magnates'. In the explanation of his actions in 1297, which he issued on 12 August, he made no reference to the community, preferring instead to refer to the 'good people' of his realm. He did not try to claim consent from the community for the tax of an eighth he tried to levy in the same year, but mendaciously stated instead that the earls and barons had agreed to it. At the same time, the term was not abandoned by the critics of the crown. In 1301 a 'bill of the prelates and nobles ... on behalf of the whole community' was presented in parliament.[16]

When Edward II came to the throne an attempt was made to resolve the political problems caused in part by the new king's fondness for Piers Gaveston, and in part by the legacy received from his father. A new clause was added to the Coronation Oath, in which the king promised to maintain the rightful laws and customs 'which the community of your realm will have chosen (*aura eslu*)', a phrase which historians have imbued with a range of meaning that would surely have mystified any contemporary. In 1309 articles similar in many respects to the *Articuli super Cartas* of 1300 were presented, according to the record, 'to our lord the king by the community of the realm in parliament'. And yet far from being a main weapon against the crown, in the Ordinances of 1311 the terminology of community was abandoned in favour of the less emotive 'the baronage'.[17]

The reasons for these changes lie in the shifting meaning of the word 'community'. It is normally assumed that under Edward I it still meant no more than the magnates, though historians have differed on the point. In 1274 proctors acting for the earls and barons were described as being messengers on behalf of the community of England.[18] Yet the Easter parliament of 1275 was attended not only by magnates, but also by knights of the shire, and a very impressive number of burgesses. It is very likely that this wider attendance of representatives was in the minds of the clerks who drafted the Statute of Westminster, and included the community as consenting to this legislation. By 1290 there was a note of caution in the grant of the aid for the marriage of the king's daughter. The magnates present made the grant 'for themselves and the community of the whole realm insofar as in them lies'. They clearly did not feel wholly confident to speak on behalf of the community as a whole. The letter of the English barons sent to the pope in 1301 betrays a similar sentiment, for it was sealed by them 'as much for ourselves as for the whole community of the said realm of England'.[19] There are interesting indications of a broad interpretation of community during Edward's dealings with the Scots when the question of the right to the throne was determined in the Great Cause. The English clerks evidently did not normally equate the community of Scotland with the nobility. The usual phraseology was 'the bishops, prelates, earls, barons, magnates, and the community of the realm of Scotland'. The magnates were certainly considered to be part of the community, but the clerks do not appear to have thought that they alone formed it.[20]

Was it then the case that the development of representation in parliament by knights of the shire, citizens and burgesses, brought with it a concept of a much broader community of the realm than had existed in the mid-thirteenth century? There was a very large number of representatives present in the Easter parliament of 1275, and this could be one reason why reference was made to the community of the land in the preamble to the Statute of Westminster. In summoning the representatives of shire and borough, the king developed the idea that they should come with full powers (*plena potestas*) on behalf of their communities. Surely an assembly of all the community representatives would amount to a gathering of the community of the realm as a whole? Such seductive logic is, unfortunately, too simple.

Representation by knights of the shire antedates the

beginnings of parliament, and was not fully integrated into parliament until after the first quarter of the fourteenth century. It was King John who first summoned knights to discuss the affairs of the realm. After he heard of the baronial plot of 1212 against him, he summoned six knights from each shire who were to receive instructions from him. Then, in 1213, four knights from each shire were asked to come 'to speak with us concerning the affairs of our realm'. This second summons presents major difficulties of timing, for no more than a week's notice was given. Yet whether or not the assembly actually met, the fact remains that John had seen fit to widen the political nation by calling knights to meet him, in a bid to weaken the position of his baronial enemies. Little may have come of this in John's reign, but the precedent was followed in 1226, when four knights were summoned from each county to discuss the interpretation of Magna Carta. That writ was cancelled, but a similar one was sent out in the next year. In 1254 knights were summoned by the regency government to discuss a grant of taxation. The writs suggested that the knights from one county would act together with those from the others, and as Holt has rightly stressed, they came on behalf of their local county communities, and not as representatives of the community of the realm as a whole. There was no suggestion that a gathering of representatives of the various county communities constituted a meeting of the community of the realm.[21]

During the period of Simon de Montfort's dominance, knights were summoned for a variety of reasons, but it was only in 1265 that the writs specified that they were to give counsel. Their presence was requested in 1258, 1261, 1264 and in 1265. In view of the number of parliaments held in this period, the record is a slender one. No chronicler considered the presence of knights worth recording. The parliament of 1265 saw, in addition to the knights, burgesses summoned for the first time. The knights seem to have played an important part, for they spent longer at parliament than was expected. This was an assembly held at a time of growing crisis for the baronial regime. Montfort's support was dwindling, and this was a gathering of his remaining supporters, hardly representative of the community of the land.

It has recently been argued by J. R. Maddicott that the relatively obscure period which followed the defeat of Simon de Montfort at Evesham in 1265 was of great significance for the development of parliament and the place of the representatives in it.[22] For the first time since 1237 a general tax was negotiated, and to do this it proved necessary to summon knights of the shire and probably burgesses with a new regularity. The argument depends on the interpretation of difficult texts: in particular, on the translation of *maiores* as the commons. There are no surviving writs of summons, but in a letter the king referred to the tax as being 'conceded as much by the magnates and knights as other laymen', and one chronicler was clear that townsmen were involved. The same author, however, was also capable of defining attendance at parliament as being by 'bishops, earls, barons, knights and free tenants of the whole realm of England', not the best way to describe a representative commons.[23] These parliaments of Henry III's final years on the throne provide important precedents for the fully representative parliament of Easter 1275.

Despite these indications that the representatives played a significant political role in the parliaments of 1268–70, it was not for many years that they were to be summoned to all parliaments, or even to a majority of parliaments. There were some fifty parliaments under Edward I, but there are only eighteen known occasions when representatives were summoned. The frequency of Edward I's demands for taxation after 1294 meant that knights of the shire and burgesses began to attend more regularly, and from 1295 the style of the writs used to summon them was fixed. They were to come with full powers on behalf of their local community to do what should be ordained by common counsel. It was, however, only very slowly that these men began to consider that they might speak on behalf of the community as a whole.

In addition to the knights and burgesses, proctors of the lower clergy were summoned fairly regularly to parliament from 1295. Like the lay representatives, they were to have full powers to act on behalf of the clergy of their diocese. Their contribution to parliament has not received as much attention as has that of the knights and burgesses, for by 1340 the clergy had established their right to discuss requests for tax grants in their own convocations, rather than in parliament. Viewed in the long term, clerical representation was a cul-de-sac off the highway leading to the modern parliament. In the immediate context of the early fourteenth century, however, the clerical proctors demonstrate the way in which Edward I succeeded in gaining a remarkably full representation of the whole realm in his major parliaments.[24]

What the representatives did in parliament in this period has never been clear. Assent to taxation was certainly important, and on occasion the king might use the knights he had summoned to assist in the task of collecting the taxes that they had helped to grant. No doubt the representatives also fulfilled a useful function in taking back news from parliament to their constituencies, but there is no indication that they played a large part in the wide range of parliamentary business.

One important area of parliamentary activity to which the representatives might be expected to have contributed was that of petitioning. Over sixty petitions presented in parliament in 1278 survive. They were not written according to any standard formula, and this suggests that the procedure was a fairly novel one. It may be that the business of petitioning was deliberately encouraged for the first time in 1275. Certainly by 1280 so many were coming in that they threatened to clog the other business of parliament, and arrangements had to be made to streamline the way they were dealt with. It was through petitions that many grievances came to the king's attention. It was not for many years, however, that it became normal for petitions to be brought to parliament by the representatives: anyone could present his own.[25]

There are hints from Edward I's later years that the representatives of shire, borough and clergy in parliament considered that they had a voice as a part of the community of the realm. In 1301 it was a knight of the shire, Henry Keighley, who was responsible for the bill critical of the crown presented in the Lincoln parliament, as the king discovered a few years later when he had Keighley imprisoned. Petitions against the papal tax collector in the Carlisle parliament of 1307 were from 'the earls, barons and the community of the land', and it is clear from the document that the earls and barons alone were not taken as representative of the whole community. It was not, however, until Edward II's reign that general petitions in parliament began to be presented by the representatives on behalf of the community. It was certainly still possible for the barons to write to the pope in 1309 in the name of the community, but in 1315 a petition from 'the people of the community of the realm' was very explicitly directed against the baronial interest. In 1320 a petition from the knights, citizens and burgesses in parliament was described by the clerk annotating the roll as being from the community of the realm. The community was rapidly evolving into the Commons.

In the Ordinances of 1311 various clauses specified that consent was to be given by the baronage in parliament. The community of the land was not mentioned. This should not be taken as an indication of a much more oligarchic attitude than had existed in the past. Earlier many would probably have considered baronial consent as consistent with consent by the community of the realm. By 1311 this was not so, and different terminology had to be used. The baronage were not claiming the right to provide consent in all matters. The Ordinances did not cover the question of how taxation was to be granted, and in 1312, in the course of complex discussions with the king, the baronial negotiators stated that they would do all they could to see that he was granted a tax 'when they will have their peers more fully with them, and the community'.[26] The magnates were beginning to think of themselves as the peerage, and of the commons as the community.

There were other significant changes to parliament from the 1290s. Largely because of the pressures of war, it ceased to meet as regularly as in the years before Edward I's departure to Gascony in 1286. There were substantial alterations to the list of the magnates who received individual summonses to attend. The lowest number was a mere 14 in October 1299; in contrast, 167 prelates and lay magnates were asked to attend at Carlisle in 1307. The list was, however, becoming increasingly standardised, and a parliamentary peerage was beginning to evolve. Not all those who were summoned attended, and of those who did, not all stayed for the full duration. In 1305 parliament, consisting of little more than the king's council, continued in session long after most of the magnates and all the representatives had departed.

The records of what took place in parliament are much fuller by Edward I's later years. They deal almost exclusively with legal matters and the hearing of petitions, but this can give a misleading impression. It was these affairs which needed to be recorded for future reference, in a way that was not necessary where decisions about the war in Scotland or other major issues of the moment were concerned. It is clear from chronicle and other sources that the business of parliament ranged widely, including such matters as grants of taxation, promulgation of legislation, and discussion of military plans and overseas affairs. Parliament should no more be defined in narrow legal terms for this period than it should under Henry III.[27]

The idea of the community of the realm appeared to be a potent one, as it developed in the first half of the thirteenth century. It lacked, however, the precision which would have enabled it to acquire real force. The sworn association of 1258, the *commune*, failed to retain its identity. The community of the realm ceased to be an expression of solidarity in

144

face of an oppressive crown. It became little more than a convenient phrase by Edward I's reign, losing the revolutionary overtones of earlier days. Parliament, in contrast, was becoming an institution, in part because of its function as a court of law. There were, by Edward I's day, parliamentary records, and although its composition was far from fixed, its functions were clearly recognisable. Parliament was, to a considerable extent, a royal creation, serving the needs of the crown. There is a temptation for historians to emphasise those elements in the medieval parliament which presage later developments. Thirteenth-century politics were not the parliamentary politics of the sixteenth or seventeenth centuries. The change in the course of the thirteenth century, however, from the ill-defined common counsel of the realm set out in Magna Carta, and the *commune* of 1258 to the parliaments of the late thirteenth and early fourteenth century was immense, as politics acquired an institutional focus. The changes did not result so much from the application of new ideas drawn from the world of the schools and universities, as from political practice and administrative convenience. No constitutional genius lay behind the evolution of what was sometimes rather creaky machinery: what took place was the result of a piecemeal process of trial and error.

CONCLUSION

HISTORIANS have often seen the thirteenth century in terms of a series of conflicts. The political events are depicted as crisis succeeding crisis: king versus barons, church versus state – this has been a staple diet. A valuable corrective to such an approach to medieval history has been inspired by the work of K. B. McFarlane. It has come to be appreciated that what most men wanted was to obtain good government, not the collapse of the system. They wanted to avoid conflict, not provoke it.

One way in which a political system can be judged is in its success in resolving conflicts and problems. For all the impression given by successive crises, the thirteenth-century record was a good one. John's reign ended, and Henry III's began, with civil war, but it was possible for a chronicler in 1263 to praise Henry III, with considerable justification, for having maintained peace.[1] With the minor exceptions of the siege of Bedford castle in 1224, and the Marshal rebellion of 1233–4 (which took place in the Welsh march), England was indeed kept free of civil war for the lengthy period from 1217 to 1263. It did not, however, prove possible to accommodate the ambition of Simon de Montfort, and to equate the full rigour of the reforming programme of 1258 with Henry III's conception of how he should rule. The country went through a severe trauma in 1264–5 with the battles of Lewes and Evesham. Recollection of the horrors of

146

civil war was no doubt a powerful force for stability in the rest of the century. Edward I's reign was spectacularly successful in providing this stability, particularly in his first two decades on the throne. There was a threat of civil war in 1297, but the country was free from domestic warfare throughout his reign. Not one single political opponent of the crown was executed during the thirteenth century, a record not to be achieved again until the nineteenth century.

How can this success be explained? It was very important that men thought it possible to achieve worthwhile ends by political rather than military means. Magna Carta set a precedent, for although they failed to bring peace in 1215, the negotiations at Runnymede showed that worthwhile concessions could be obtained from the crown. The development of parliament provided a suitable forum for the discussion and resolution of grievances. The process of negotiating taxes was particularly important, for the king's subjects were provided with a means to extract concessions. The need to obtain general consent compelled the crown to summon representatives to parliament with increasing regularity, so widening the political nation. With changes in the social structure, notably a weakening of the bonds between lords and tenants, the politically influential magnates found it increasingly necessary to ensure that the needs of groups in addition to their own élite were met. What was meant by the community of the realm altered as the century progressed, but the phrase, imprecise as it was, did reflect a genuine sense of national unity.

The problems that were faced varied immensely. Different issues were important at different times. The jockeying for power of court factions was a factor for instability, particularly when the process of giving out royal patronage was mismanaged, as under Henry III and Edward II. Grants to foreigners were particularly resented: anti-alien sentiment was an important element in politics. Above all, the Poitevins, headed by Henry III's half-brothers, were the object of dislike and envy. The way in which local government operated was of great concern to the knightly classes. The king's ambitions abroad and his demands for military service were important in 1214, and again in 1297, but the crisis of 1258 took place against a different kind of background, in which the costs of Henry III's plans to obtain the Sicilian throne for his second son were only one element among many. Royal demands for taxation were significant, but Henry III's failure to negotiate any taxes between 1237 and 1269 reduced the importance of this element in the political equation in the central years of the century.

There are no easy answers to the problems posed by the thirteenth century. This book began by arguing that English politics scarcely existed prior to this period, for previously English affairs had been too closely bound up with those of Normandy and the other continental possessions. Yet it would be wrong to treat England too much in isolation. It has been suggested that Magna Carta was far from unique, that it finds parallels in the Golden Bull of Hungary of 1222, or the *Statutum in Favorem Principum* of 1231 in Germany.[2] Those documents do not have the special qualities of Magna Carta, with its demands for liberties extending to all free men, but they show that some other monarchies faced similar problems to the English. The Spanish kingdoms provide with the *cortes* interesting parallels to English parliamentary developments, and even the autocratic Frederick II held a parliament at Messina in Sicily in 1234. The English *commune* of 1258 finds parallels with the Commune of Acre two decades earlier. The financial problems which led the English monarchs to negotiate grants with their subjects, and to borrow money from Italian merchants, were certainly not unique. The arguments from necessity, the terminology of *plena potestas*, were part of a common heritage. The church was a European-wide institution, and the problems it faced in England cannot be treated in isolation. The contribution of foreigners to English political life in the thirteenth century was far from being the wholly negative one implied by the chronicler Matthew Paris. The experience of men such as Peter of Savoy, and indeed Simon de Montfort himself, on a wider stage cannot be ignored.

One of the most difficult problems is to determine how far events and institutions were affected by the ideas and conceptions of the age. One historian of France, J. R. Strayer, wrote that 'I have not discussed the political theories or the theological controversies of the learned because they had little effect on events'.[3] It is not easy to share such blunt assurance. Political activity had to operate at certain levels within a framework of ideas which was the product of scholarly activity. The extent to which Simon de Montfort was influenced by Robert Grosseteste's ideas can never be calculated, but the theoretical dimension cannot be ignored, even though problems of political theory were of peripheral interest to most thirteenth-century scholars. The *Song of Lewes* shows the way in which one author applied his theoretical ideas about the nature of kingship to events in England. At another level, it can be shown that some of the terminology adopted for summoning representatives to parliament derived from Roman law. Theory, however, should not be given precedence over practice. The fact that phrases such as *plena potestas* were used by well-educated royal clerks does not mean that kings and nobles considered that they were bound by principles drawn from Roman law.

All periods can be regarded as formative in different ways, but the claims of the thirteenth century are especially strong. Magna Carta and the early development of parliament alone ensure the period a notable place in English history. There was much more of significance in the century in political terms, most notably the affirmation of principles of consultation and consent. The achievements were not the work of individuals alone: for all the imprecision of the concept, full credit must go to the community of the realm.

REFERENCES

INTRODUCTION

1. F. M. Powicke, *King Henry III and the Lord Edward* (Oxford: Clarendon Press, 1947); *The Thirteenth Century 1216–1307*, second ed. (Oxford: Clarendon Press, 1962); R. C. Stacey, *Politics, Policy and Finance under Henry III 1216–1245* (Oxford: Clarendon Press, 1987), p. vii.
2. H. G. Richardson and G. O. Sayles, *The English Parliament in the Middle Ages* (London: Hambledon Press, 1981) is a collection of their most important papers. See also G. O. Sayles, *The King's Parliament of England* (London: Edward Arnold, 1975).
3. M. Prestwich, *Edward I* (London: Methuen, 1988) is the most recent study of the reign.
4. J. R. Maddicott, *Thomas of Lancaster* (Oxford: Clarendon Press, 1970), and J. R. S. Phillips, *Aymer de Valence, earl of Pembroke* (Oxford: Clarendon Press, 1972), pioneered the reinterpretation of Edward II's reign.

1 KINGSHIP

1. T. Wright (ed.), *The Political Songs of England* (London: Camden Society, 1839), pp. 72–124.
2. C. F. Slade (ed.), *Pipe Roll, 12 John* (London: Pipe Roll Society, new series. xxvi, 1949), p. 139.
3. M. Prestwich, *War, Politics and Finance under Edward I* (London: Faber & Faber, 1972), p. 236.
4. M. Prestwich (ed.), *Documents Illustrating the Crisis of 1297–98 in*

England (London: Camden Society, 4th series, xxiv, 1980), p. 107.

5. W. Stubbs *The Constitutional History of England*, vol. II, fourth ed. (Oxford: Clarendon Press, 1906), p. 158n.

6. Prestwich (ed.), *Documents Illustrating the Crisis of 1297–98*, p. 140.

7. Ibid., p. 122.

8. Ibid., p. 134.

9. Thomas Aquinas argued that as a prince was the head of the law, he could not be coerced by it: the law only has coercive force from the power of the prince. He also made it clear that those who make laws for others should keep them themselves. See B. Tierney, 'Bracton on Government', *Speculum*, xxxviii (1963), 304.

10. Quoted by G. L. Harriss, *King, Parliament and Public Finance in Medieval England to 1369* (Oxford: Clarendon Press, 1975), p. 22.

11. W. Stubbs (ed.), *Select Charters*, ninth ed. (Oxford: Clarendon Press, 1921), pp. 276–8.

12. M. T. Clanchy, *England and its Rulers 1066–1272* (Glasgow: Fontana, 1983), p. 224; see also R. W. Southern, *Robert Grosseteste* (Oxford: Clarendon Press, 1986), pp. 268–9.

13. E. Peters, *The Shadow King* (New Haven: Yale University Press, 1970), p. 157. I owe the suggestion that Montfort may have had Sancho iv in mind to a paper by Professor R. C. Stacey, to be published in P. R. Coss and S. D. Lloyd (eds.), *Thirteenth Century England III: Proceedings of the Newcastle upon Tyne Conference, 1989*. Interestingly, Wykes in his chronicle used the phrase '*inutilem et insufficientem*' of Henry iii's rule in 1258: H. R. Luard (ed.), *Annales Monastici*, vol. iv (London: Rolls ser. 1869), pp. 118–19.

14. H. G. Hewlett (ed.), *Chronica Rogeri de Wendover*, vol. iii (London: Rolls ser., 1889), p. 76.

15. Stubbs, *Select Charters*, p. 278; R. V. Turner, *The King and his Courts: the role of John and Henry III in the administration of Justice* (Ithaca: Cornell University Press, 1968), pp. 174–9.

16. W. J. Whittaker (ed.), *The Mirror of Justices* (London: Selden Society, 1895), pp. 6–7; G. O. Sayles, *The Functions of the Medieval Parliament of England* (London: Hambledon Press, 1988), p. 19.

17. Stubbs, *Constitutional History*, vol. ii, p. 133.

18. H. G. Richardson and G. O. Sayles, *The Governance of Medieval*

England (Edinburgh: Edinburgh University Press, 1963), 144–6, citing G. E. Woodbine (ed), Henry de Bracton, *De legibus et consuetudines Angliae* (New Haven: Yale Historical Publications, 1915–42), vol. ii, p. 110.

19. J. C. Holt, *Magna Carta* (Cambridge: Cambridge University Press, 1965), provides the best commentary on the Charter, which is printed, with translation, on pp. 316–37.
20. D. A. Carpenter, 'Chancellor Ralph de Neville and Plans of Political Reform, 1215–1258', in P. R. Coss and S. D. Lloyd (eds.), *Thirteenth Century England II: Proceedings of the Newcastle upon Tyne Conference, 1987* (Woodbridge: Boydell Press, 1988), pp. 69–80.
21. R. F. Treharne and I. J. Sanders (eds.), *Documents of the Baronial Movement of Reform and Rebellion, 1258–1267* (Oxford: Clarendon Press, 1973), pp. 215, 225.
22. J. R. Maddicott, 'Edward and the Lessons of Baronial Reform: Local Government, 1258–80', in P. R. Coss and S. D. Lloyd (eds.) *Thirteenth Century England I: Proceedings of the Newcastle upon Tyne Conference, 1985* (Woodbridge: Boydell Press, 1986), pp. 1–30; D. W. Sutherland, *Quo Warranto Proceedings in the Reign of Edward I, 1278–1294* (Oxford: Clarendon Press, 1963).
23. For the politics of Edward's later years, see Prestwich, *Edward I*, pp. 517–55.
24. Treharne and Sanders (eds.), *Documents of the Baronial Movement*, pp. 288–9.

2 THE ARISTOCRACY

1. Stubbs, *Constitutional History of England*, vol. ii, pp. 311–12; K. B. McFarlane, *The Nobility of Later Medieval England* (Oxford: Clarendon Press, 1973), p. 3.
2. K. B. McFarlane, 'Had Edward I a "Policy" towards the Earls?', *History*, l (1965), 145–59, reprinted in his *The Nobility of Later Medieval England*, pp. 248–67.
3. J. C. Holt, *The Northerners: a Study in the Reign of King John* (Oxford: Clarendon Press, 1961), pp. 35–60, discusses these complex problems.
4. S. L. Waugh, 'Tenure to Contract: lordship and clientage in thirteenth-century England', *English Historical Review*, ci (1986), 826.
5. G. G. Simpson, 'The *Familia* of Roger de Quincy, earl of

Winchester and Constable of Scotland', in K. Stringer (ed.), *Essays on the Nobility of Medieval Scotland* (Edinburgh: John Donald, 1985), pp. 102–29.

6. Prestwich (ed.), *Documents Illustrating the Crisis of 1297–98*, pp. 57–8.
7. Prestwich, *War, Politics and Finance under Edward I*, pp. 64–5.
8. Holt, *The Northerners*, pp. 55–6, 59.
9. S. L. Waugh, 'Tenure to Contract: lordship and clientage in Thirteenty-Century England', pp. 829, 832; S. Lloyd, *English Society and the Crusade, 1216–1307* (Oxford: Clarendon Press, 1988), pp. 81, 85; *Calendar of Inquisitions Miscellaneous, Vol. I, 1219–1307* (London: HMSO, 1916), p. 216.
10. Stacey, *Politics, Policy and Finance under Henry III*, pp. 38–9.
11. Holt, *The Northerners*, pp. 65–7.
12. D. T. Williams, 'Simon de Montfort and his Adherents', in W. M. Ormrod (ed.), *England in the Thirteeenth Century* (Harlaxton: Harlaxton College, 1985), p. 173.
13. Powicke, *King Henry III and the Lord Edward*, vol. i, p. 397.
14. N. Denholm-Young, *Seigneurial Administration in England* (Oxford: Oxford University Press, 1937), pp. 167–8; Phillips, *Aymer de Valence, earl of Pembroke*, p. 316.
15. J. R. V. Barker, *The Tournament in England 1100–1400* (Woodbridge: Boydell Press, 1986), pp. 45–69.
16. Holt, *Magna Carta*, pp. 107–8; Prestwich, *War, Politics and Finance under Edward I*, pp. 236–7.
17. D. A. Carpenter, 'King, Magnates and Society: the personal rule of King Henry III, 1234–1258', *Speculum* lx (1985), 52–7.
18. *Close Rolls, Henry III, 1251–1253* (London: HMSO, 1927), p. 7; *Calendar of Patent Rolls, 1247–58* (London: HMSO, 1908), p. 529; H. R. Luard (ed.), *Annales Monastici* (Rolls Ser., 1864–9), vol. i, p. 175.
19. S. Painter, *The Reign of King John* (Baltimore: Johns Hopkins Press, 1949), p. 235.
20. M. Altschul, *A Baronial Family in Medieval England: the Clares* (Baltimore: Johns Hopkins Press, 1965), pp. 80–110.
21. The first quotation is by G. Duby, cited by J. Gillingham, 'War and Chivalry in the History of William the Marshal', in Coss and Lloyd (eds.) *Thirteenth Century England II*, p. 6; the second from K. B. McFarlane, *The Nobility of Later Medieval England*, p. 41.
22. Gillingham, 'War and Chivalry in the History of William the Marshal', pp. 1–13.

3   THE COUNTY COMMUNITY

1. S. Reynolds, *Kingdoms and Communities in Western Europe, 900–1300* (Oxford: Clarendon Press, 1984); J. R. Maddicott, 'Magna Carta and the Local Community 1215–1259', *Past and Present*, cii (1984) 25–65; Stubbs, *Constitutional History*, vol. ii, pp. 194–5; R. C. Palmer, *The County Courts of Medieval England, 1150–1350* (Princeton N.J.: Princeton University Press, 1982).

2. D. A. Carpenter, 'The Decline of the Curial Sheriff in England', *English Historical Review*, xci (1976), 1–32.

3. Palmer, *County Courts*, pp. 11–27, 56–88; the quotations are from pp. 88, 119.

4. G. T. Lapsley, *'Buzones', English Historical Review*, xlvii (1923), 177–93, 545–67; Palmer, *County Courts*, pp. 132–3; P. Coss, 'Knighthood and the Early Thirteenth-Century County Court', in Coss and Lloyd (eds.), *Thirteenth Century England II*, pp. 45–57.

5. Palmer, *County Courts*, p. 135; Maddicott, 'Magna Carta and the Local Community', p. 33.

6. Ibid., pp. 27–9.

7. Ibid., p. 62.

8. D. T. Williams, 'Simon de Montfort and his Adherents', pp. 166–77.

9. Prestwich, *Edward I*, pp. 287, 426.

10. J. R. Maddicott, 'Parliament and the Constituencies', in R. G. Davies and J. H. Denton (eds.), *The English Parliament in the Middle Ages* (Manchester: Manchester University Press, 1981), p. 69.

11. N. Saul, *Scenes from Provincial Life* (Oxford: Clarendon Press, 1986), pp. 61, 191–2.

12. G. Platts, *Land and People in Medieval Lincolnshire* (Lincoln: History of Lincolnshire Committee, 1985), pp. 278–9.

13. T. Stapleton (ed.), *Liber de Antiquis Legibus* (London: Camden Soc., xxxiv, 1846), p. 61; Powicke, *King Henry III and the Lord Edward*, vol. ii, p. 509.

14. Holt, *Magna Carta*, pp. 58–9.

15. The major contributions to the thirteenth-century debate have been provided by R. F. Treharne, 'The Knights in the Period of Reform and Revolution', *Bulletin of the Institute of Historical Research*, xxi (1946), 1–12; P. R. Coss, 'Sir Geoffrey de Langley and the Crisis of the Knightly Class in Thirteenth-Century England', *Past and Present*, lxviii (1975), 3–37; D. A. Carpenter,

'Was there a crisis of the knightly class in the thirteenth century? The Oxfordshire evidence', *English Historical Review*, xcv (1980) 723–52; E. King, 'Large and Small Landowners in Thirteenth-Century England', *Past and Present*, xlvii (1970), 26–50. Overall numbers were discussed by N. Denholm-Young, *Collected Papers on Mediaeval Subjects* (Oxford: Blackwell, 1946), pp. 56–67; for a recent comment, J. Quick, 'The Number and Distribution of Knights in Thirteenth Century England: The Evidence of the Grand Assize', Coss and Lloyd (eds.) *Thirteenth Century England I*, pp. 114–23.

4 THE CHURCH

1. For analysis of the bishops under Henry iii, see M. Gibbs and J. Lang, *Bishops and Reform 1215–1272* (London: Oxford University Press, 1934), pp. 1–52.
2. Holt, *Magna Carta*, pp. 137–8; Richardson and Sayles, *The Governance of Medieval England*, p. 359; but for a defence of Wendover, see Clanchy, *England and its Rulers*, p. 194. The fullest discussion of Innocent iii's role is in C. R. Cheney, *Innocent III and England* (*Papste und Pappstum*, vol. ix, Stuttgart: Anton Hiersemann, 1976).
3. Holt, *Magna Carta*, 228–9.
4. F. A. Cazel, Jr., 'The Legates Guala and Pandulf', Coss and Lloyd (eds.), *Thirteenth Century England II*, pp. 15–21.
5. Hewlett (ed.), *Chronica Rogeri de Wendover*, vol. iii, pp. 75–87; T. Wright (ed.), *The Chronicle of Pierre de Langtoft* (Rolls series, 1868), vol. ii, pp. 290–3.
6. F. M. Powicke and C. R. Cheney (eds.), *Councils and Synods II A.D. 1205–1313* (Oxford: Clarendon Press, 1964), part I, pp. 472, 477–8, 539–48.
7. C. Bémont, *Simon de Montfort*, tr. E. F. Jacob (Oxford: Clarendon Press, 1930), pp. 42–5; R. W. Southern, *Robert Grosseteste*, pp. 289–90.
8. M. Jancey (ed.), *St Thomas Cantilupe, Bishop of Hereford. Essays in his honour* (Hereford: Friends of Hereford Cathedral, 1982).
9. C. Tyerman, *England and the Crusades 1095–1588* (Chicago: Chicago University Press, 1988), pp. 133–51, discusses political crusading in thirteenth-century England. For the crusade in this period, see also S. Lloyd, *English Society and the Crusade, 1216–1307*.

10. Prestwich, *Edward I*, pp. 249–58, 414–20. For the fullest discussion of the clergy in 1297, see J. H. Denton, *Robert Winchelsey and the Crown, 1294–1313* (Cambridge: Cambridge University Press, 1980), pp. 100–35.
11. Prestwich, *Edward I*, pp. 541–6; C. M. Fraser, *A History of Anthony Bek* (Oxford: Clarendon Press, 1957).
12. Powicke and Cheney (eds.), *Councils and Synods II*, part I, pp. 477–9; for an important discussion of the issues, J. W. Gray, 'The Church and Magna Carta in the Century after Runnymede', T. W. Moody (ed.), *Historical Studies VI* (New York: Barnes and Noble, 1968), pp. 23–38.
13. Denton, *Robert Winchelsey and the Crown*, pp. 112–13, 116–17, 146–7, 154–5; Prestwich (ed.), *Documents Illustrating the Crisis of 1297–98*, pp. 43–4, 55–8, 142–4.
14. J. R. Strayer, 'The Laicization of French and English Society in the Thirteenth Century', in his *Medieval Statecraft and the Perspectives of History* (Princeton: Princeton University Press, 1971), pp. 251–65.
15. R. V. Turner, *The English Judiciary in the Age of Glanvill and Bracton, c.1176–1239* (Cambridge: Cambridge University Press, 1985), p. 291.
16. I give Strayer's translation, *op. cit.* p. 260, See also Treharne and Sanders (eds.), *Documents of the Baronial Movement*, pp. 320–1.

5 ENGLISHMEN AND FOREIGNERS

1. Powicke, *King Henry III and the Lord Edward*, vol. i, pp. 161, 297, 384; Clanchy, *England and its Rulers, 1066–1272*; D. A. Carpenter, 'What Happened in 1258?', in J. Gillingham and J. C. Holt (eds.), *War and Government in the Middle Ages* (Woodbridge: Boydell Press, 1984), pp. 106–119; H. Ridgeway, 'King Henry III and the "Aliens", 1236–1272', in Coss and Lloyd (eds.), *Thirteenth Century England II*, pp. 81–92; H. Ridgeway, 'Foreign Favourites and Henry III's Problems of Patronage, 1247–1258', *English Historical Review*, civ (1989), 590–610.
2. J. O. Halliwell (ed.), *The Chronicle of William de Rishanger* (London: Camden Soc., 1840), pp. 17–18; N. Denholm-Young, *Vita Edwardi Secundi* (London: Nelson, 1957), p. 63; Southern, *Robert Grosseteste*, p. 241; Stacey, *Politics, Policy and Finance*, pp. 169–70.

3. J. Gillingham, *Richard the Lionheart* (London: Methuen, 1978), p. 50.

4. R. R. Davies, *Conquest, Coexistence and Change: Wales, 1063–1415* (Oxford: Clarendon Press, 1987), pp. 252, 274; Wright (ed.), *Langtoft*, vol. ii, pp. 220–1.

5. F. W. D. Brie (ed.), *The Brut* vol. ii (Early English Text Soc., 1908), p. 220.

6. Wright (ed.), *Political Songs*, pp. 63–8; P. Rickard, *Britain in Medieval French Literature 1100–1500* (Cambridge: Cambridge University Press, 1956).

7. Stubbs (ed.), *Select Charters*, p. 357.

8. Powicke and Cheney (eds.), *Councils and Synods II*, part I, p. 393.

9. For the fall of Fawkes, and the politics of this period, see D. A. Carpenter, 'The Fall of Hubert de Burgh', *Journal of British Studies*, xix (1980), 1–17.

10. Luard (ed.), *Chronicon Rogeri de Wendover*, vol. iii, pp. 58, 75.

11. H. R. Luard (ed.), *Matthew Paris, Chronica Majora*, ed. H. R. Luard (Rolls Ser., 1872–84), vol. v, pp. 185, 227, 316, 398, 469, 569.

12. For a recent discussion, see Ridgeway, 'King Henry III and the "Aliens", 1236–1272', in Coss and Lloyd (eds.), *Thirteenth Century England II*, pp. 81–92.

13. Luard (ed.), *Matthew Paris, Chronica Majora*, vol. v, pp. 283, 343, 344–5.

14. Ibid., vol. iv, p. 633; vol. v, pp. 17–18, 54, 83, 265.

15. R. F. Treharne, *The Baronial Plan of Reform 1258–1263* (Manchester: Manchester University Press, 1932), p. 76. Powicke, *King Henry III and the Lord Edward*, vol. i, p. 384.

16. Luard (ed.), *Annales Monastici*, vol. i, p. 164; Luard (ed.), *Matthew Paris, Chronica Majora*, vol. v, p. 689; Carpenter, 'What Happened in 1258?', pp. 106–9. See also Ridgeway's articles, cited above, note 1. Powicke, *King Henry III and the Lord Edward*, vol. i, p. 384 n. 2, does not accept the Tewkesbury account of Bigod's speech, pointing out that it is not supported by record evidence. Such an argument from silence is dangerous: parliamentary speeches were not recorded at this period. Carpenter suggests that the Tewkesbury chronicler made use of a newsletter from the Westminster parliament.

17. H. Ellis (ed.), *Chronica Johannis de Oxenedes* (Rolls Ser., 1859), pp. 224–5; H. T. Riley (ed.), *Johannis de Trokelowe et Henrici de Blaneford Chronica et Annales 1259–1296* (Rolls Ser., 1866), 5;

Treharne and Sanders (eds.) *Documents of the Baronial Movement*, p. 289.

18. Treharne and Sanders, *Documents of the Baronial Movement*, pp. 208–9, 268–79, 298–9; W. Stubbs (ed.), *Chronicles of the reigns of Edward I and Edward II* (Rolls Ser., 1882), vol. i, p. 61; Wright (ed.), *Political Songs*, pp. 86, 101, 110.
19. Luard (ed.), *Annales Monastici*, vol. i, pp. 179–80.
20. Ridgeway, 'King Henry III and the "Aliens"', p. 91.
21. M. Prestwich, 'Royal Patronage under Edward I', in Coss and Lloyd (eds.), *Thirteenth Century England I*, pp. 41–52.
22. Prestwich, *Edward I*, p. 383 and note. In a letter of 1262 Peter de Montfort referred to the Welsh as 'the men of the Welsh tongue': W. W. Shirley (ed.), *Royal Letters, Henry III* (Rolls Ser., 1862–6), vol. ii, p. 230.
23. Holt, *The Northerners*, pp. 85–6.
24. Stubbs (ed.), *Select Charters*, pp. 289, 294, 377; Stacey, *Politics, Policy and Finance*, pp. 132–59; Prestwich, *Edward I*, pp. 343–6.
25. R. W. Kaeuper, *Bankers to the Crown: the Riccardi of Lucca and Edward I* (Princeton: Princeton University Press, 1973); M. Prestwich, 'Italian Merchants in Late Thirteenth and Early Fourteenth Century England', *The Dawn of Modern Banking* (Yale: Yale University Press, 1979), pp. 77–104.
26. H. MacKenzie, 'The Anti-foreign Movement in England, 1231–32', in C. H. Taylor (ed.), *Anniversary Essays in Medieval History by Students of C. H. Haskins* (Boston and New York: Houghton Mifflin, 1927), pp. 183–203; Stacey, *Politics, Policy and Finance*, p. 137; Luard (ed.), *Annales Monastici*, vol. i, pp. 487–91; Prestwich, *Edward I*, pp. 551–2.

6 MILITARY SERVICE

1. The fullest treatment of the subject is provided by M. R. Powicke, *Military Obligation in Medieval England* (Oxford: Clarendon Press, 1962), pp. 63–117.
2. Holt, *The Northerners*, pp. 88–100, for a full discussion of the demands for service in 1213 and 1214.
3. Stacey, *Politics, Policy and Finance under Henry III*, pp. 170, 190–2.
4. For demands for service under Edward I, see Prestwich, *War, Politics and Finance under Edward I*, pp. 67–91.

5. The reductions in quotas are discussed and analysed by I. J. Sanders, *Feudal Military Service in England* (Oxford: Clarendon Press, 1956), pp. 50–90.

6. Distraint of knighthood under Henry III is discussed by Powicke, *Military Obligation in Medieval England*, pp. 63–81; *Close Rolls, Henry III, 1251–3* (London: HMSO, 1927), pp. 490–1, 502; *Calendar of Patent Rolls, 1247–58* (London: HMSO, 1908), p. 236; Shirley (ed.), *Royal Letters, Henry III*, vol. ii, p. 102.

7. See Prestwich, *War, Politics and Finance under Edward I*, pp. 83–90.

8. D. M. Stenton (ed.), *Pipe Roll 5 Richard I* (London: Pipe Roll Society, New Series III, 1927), p. 148; F. A. Cazel Jr. (ed.), *Roll of Divers Accounts for the Early Years of Henry III* (London: Pipe Roll Society, New Series xliv, 1982), p. 34; T. D. Hardy (ed.), *Rotuli de Liberatis ac de Misis et Praestitis* (London: Record Commission, 1844), p. 223.

9. Prestwich, *War, Politics and Finance under Edward I*, pp. 71–4.

10. Ibid., pp. 92–113. See also Powicke, *Military Obligation in Medieval England*, pp. 82–95, 118–33.

7 TAXATION

1. S. K. Mitchell, *Taxation in Medieval England* (New Haven: Yale University Press, 1951), pp. 156–235; J. G. Edwards, 'The *Plena Potestas* of English Parliamentary Representatives', in E. B. Fryde and E. Miller (eds.), *Historical Studies of the English Parliament* (Cambridge: Cambridge University Press, 1970), pp. 136–49; G. Post, *Studies in Medieval Legal Thought* (Princeton: Princeton University Press, 1964); G. L. Harriss, *King, Parliament and Public Finance in England to 1369* (Oxford: Clarendon Press, 1975).

2. Stacey, *Politics, Policy and Finance under Henry III*, p. 207; Prestwich, *War, Politics and Finance under Edward I*, p. 178.

3. Stubbs (ed.), *Select Charters*, p. 278.

4. Stubbs (ed.), *Select Charters*, pp. 294–5. Holt, *Magna Carta*, 222, considers that clause 12 of Magna Carta ignores the tax of 1207, but although it does not specifically deal with this type of taxation of movables and rents, it was surely the main form of tax to which the provisions about consent were intended to apply.

5. Stubbs (ed.), *Select Charters*, pp. 349, 356, 358.
6. Mitchell, *Taxation in Medieval England*, pp. 196, 201.
7. Harriss, *King, Parliament and Public Finance*, pp. 33–5.
8. Stubbs (ed.), *Select Charters*, pp. 349, 366.
9. Harriss, *King, Parliament and Public Finance*, pp. 35–6.
10. For this tax, see Stacey, *Politics, Policy and Finance under Henry III*, pp. 112–14; Luard (ed.), *Matthew Paris, Chronica Majora*, vol. iii, pp. 380–4; *Curia Regis Rolls, XV, 1233–37* (London: HMSO, 1972), pp. lvi–livii.
11. Luard (ed.), *Matthew Paris, Chronica Majora*, vol. iv, pp. 362–3, 372–3. For the latest discussion of this crisis, see Stacey, *Politics, Policy and Finance under Henry III*, pp. 247–54.
12. Mitchell, *Studies in Taxation under John and Henry III* (New Haven: Yale University Press, 1914), pp. 87, 169–71, 270, 277–8.
13. Ibid., pp. 289–90.
14. J. R. Maddicott, 'The Crusade Taxation of 1268–1270 and the Development of Parliament', in Coss and Lloyd (eds.), *Thirteenth Century England II*, pp. 93–117.
15. For the crisis of 1297, see Prestwich (ed.), *Documents Illustrating the Crisis of 1297–98*, pp. 1–37.
16. Powicke and Cheney (eds.), *Councils and Synods II*, part II, pp. 1191, 1197.
17. Prestwich, *Edward I*, pp. 522–30. For full details of the lay taxes under Edward I, see J. F. Willard, *Parliamentary Taxes on Personal Property, 1290 to 1334* (Cambridge, Mass.: Medieval Academy of America, 1934).
18. Stubbs (ed.), *Select Charters*, p. 472.
19. Harriss, *King, Parliament and Public Finance*, pp. 68–72; Mitchell, *Taxation in Medieval England*, pp. 58–61.
20. Customs duties are discussed by T. H. Lloyd, *The English Wool Trade in the Middle Ages* (Cambridge: Cambridge University Press, 1977), pp. 60–3, 75–7, 106; Prestwich, *Edward I*, pp. 99–100, 402, 530.
21. Wright (ed.), *Political Songs*, p. 184.
22. F. A. Cazel, Jr. and A. P. Cazel (eds.), *Lay Subsidy Rolls, 1225, 1232* (London: Pipe Roll Society, New Series XLV, 1983), p. 24.
23. Prestwich, *Edward I*, pp. 410–12, 421.

References

8   PARLIAMENT AND COMMUNITY

1. W. Stubbs (ed.), *Historical Works of Gervase of Canterbury* (Rolls Ser., 1879–80), vol. ii, p. 96; Stubbs (ed.), *Select Charters*, pp. 276, 278.
2. Stubbs (ed.), *Select Charters*, pp. 356, 358.
3. Luard (ed.), *Matthew Paris, Chronica Majora*, vol. iii, pp. 74, 364; Carpenter, 'Chancellor Ralph de Neville and Plans of Political Reform, 1215–1258', in Coss and Lloyd (eds.), *Thirteenth Century England II*, p. 70.
4. Powicke and Cheney (eds.), *Councils and Synods, II*, part i, pp. 389, 392; Luard (ed.), *Matthew Paris, Chronica Majora*, vol. iv, pp. 366–8; vol. v, p. 83.
5. Treharne, *Baronial Plan of Reform*, p. 67; Clanchy, *England and its Rulers*, pp. 267–70.
6. W. Stubbs (ed.), *Select Charters*, pp. 387–8; Treharne and Sanders (eds.), *Documents of the Baronial Movement*, pp. 92–3, 100–1, 116, 156–7.
7. Luard (ed.), *Annales Monastici*, vol. i, p. 471; Stapleton (ed.), *Liber de Antiquis Legibus*, p. 61.
8. Wright (ed.), *Political Songs*, pp. 110–11, 115; Powicke, *King Henry III and the Lord Edward*, vol. ii, p. 509. I have modified Powicke's 'commonalty' to 'community'.
9. This view has been set out in a great many publications, but see in particular G. O. Sayles, *The King's Parliament of England* (London: Arnold, 1975), and most recently, *The Functions of the Medieval Parliament of England* (London: Hambledon Press, 1988). Many of the papers he wrote jointly with H. G. Richardson are republished in their *The English Parliament in the Middle Ages*.
10. F. W. Maitland (ed.), *Memoranda de Parliamento, 1305* (Rolls Ser. 1893).
11. See R. F. Treharne, 'Parliament in the Reign of Henry III', in Fryde and Miller (eds.), *Historical Studies of the English Parliament*, vol. i, pp. 70–6; Sayles, *King's Parliament of England*, pp. 39–45.
12. Luard (ed.), *Matthew Paris, Chronica Majora*, vol. v, pp. 493–5.
13. Treharne and Sanders (eds.), *Documents of the Baronial Movement*, pp. 105, 111; Sayles, *Functions of the Medieval Parliament*, pp. 95–6.
14. Treharne and Sanders (eds.), *Documents of the Baronial Movement*, p. 157; Stubbs (ed.), *Select Charters*, p. 442.

15. Prestwich (ed.), *Documents illustrating the Crisis of 1297–98*, pp. 115–17, 159–60.
16. Ibid., pp. 122, 129; E. L. G. Stones (ed.), *Anglo-Scottish Relations 1174–1328* (London: Nelson, 1965), p. 107; Sayles, *Functions of the Medieval Parliament*, pp. 243–4.
17. M. Prestwich, 'Parliament and the Community of the Realm in Fourteenth-Century England', in A. Cosgrove and J. I. McGuire (eds.), *Parliament and Community* (Belfast: Appletree Press, 1983), pp. 7–9.
18. Sayles, *Functions of the Medieval Parliament*, p. 137.
19. Stubbs (ed.), *Select Charters*, p. 472; Stubbs (ed.), *Chronicles, Edward I and Edward II*, vol. i, p. 125.
20. E. L. G. Stones and G. G. Simpson (eds.), *Edward I and the Throne of Scotland 1290–1296* (Oxford: Clarendon Press, 1978), vol. ii, p. 20. Note, however, the reference on p. 101, note 2, to the use of *la commune del reaume Descoce* as an apparent alternative to *les gardeins Descoce*.
21. J. C. Holt, 'The Prehistory of Parliament', in Davies and Denton (eds.), *The English Parliament in the Middle Ages*, pp. 1–28.
22. J. R. Maddicott, 'The Crusade Taxation of 1268–1270 and the Development of Parliament', in Coss and Lloyd (eds.), *Thirteenth Century England II*, pp. 93–117.
23. *Close rolls 1268–72* (London: HMSO, 1938), 245; Stapleton (ed.), *Liber de Antiquis Legibus*, p. 122.
24. J. H. Denton, 'The Clergy and Parliament in the Thirteenth and Fourteenth Centuries', in Denton and Davies (eds.), *The English Parliament in the Middle Ages*, pp. 88–108; J. H. Denton and J. P. Dooley, *Representatives of the Lower Clergy in Parliament 1295–1340* (Woodbridge: Boydell Press, 1987).
25. J. R. Maddicott, 'Parliament and the Constituencies', in Davies and Denton (eds.), *The English Parliament in the Middle Ages*, pp. 61–87.
26. Prestwich, 'Parliament and the Community of the Realm in fourteenth century England', pp. 5–24.
27. For parliament under Edward I, Prestwich, *Edward I*, pp. 436–68; A. L. Brown, *The Governance of Late Medieval England* (London: Arnold, 1989), pp. 165–9.

CONCLUSION

1. D. A. Carpenter, 'An Unknown Obituary of King Henry III from the Year 1263', in Ormrod (ed.), *England in the Thirteenth Century*, pp. 45–51.
2. Holt, *Magna Carta*, pp. 21–2.
3. J. R. Strayer, *The Reign of Philip the Fair* (Princeton, N.J.: Princeton University Press, 1980), p. xiii.

SELECT BIBLIOGRAPHY

THIS BIBLIOGRAPHY is designed to provide an introductory guide to secondary works relevant to thirteenth-century England, especially those that are historiographically significant and illustrate recent trends in scholarship. Fuller bibliographies can be found in many of the books cited. B. Wilkinson, *The High Middle Ages in England 1154–1377* (Cambridge University Press, 1978), is a useful bibliography for works published up to that date. For comprehensive listing of more recent works the reader should consult The Royal Historical Society's annual *Bibliography of British and Irish History*.

D. A. Carpenter, 'The Decline of the Curial Sheriff in England 1194–1258', *English Historical Review*, xci (1976), pp. 1–32 – crucial study of local administration under Henry III.

D. A. Carpenter, 'What Happened in 1258?', in J. Gillingham and J. C. Holt (eds.), *War and Government in the Middle Ages* (Woodbridge: Boydell and Brewer, 1984), pp. 106–19 – revision of established views.

D. A. Carpenter, 'King, Magnates and Society: the personal rule of King Henry III, 1234–1258', *Speculum*, lx (1985), pp. 39–70 – important reassessment of Henry III's kingship.

M. T. Clanchy, *England and its Rulers, 1066–1272* (Glasgow: Fontana, 1983) – challenging textbook.

P. R. Coss and S. D. Lloyd (eds.), *Thirteenth Century England I: Proceedings of the Newcastle upon Tyne Conference 1985* (Woodbridge: Boydell Press, 1986, 1988).

P. R. Coss and S. D. Lloyd (eds.), *Thirteenth Century England II: Proceedings of the Newcastle upon Tyne Conference 1987* (Woodbridge: Boydell Press, 1986, 1988) – important collections of articles. See in particular Maddicott and Ridgeway in vol. *i*, and Coss, Carpenter, Ridgeway, and Maddicott in vol. *ii*. A third volume is due in 1990.

R. G. Davies and J. H. Denton (eds.), *The English Parliament in the Middle Ages* (Manchester: Manchester University Press, 1981) – valuable collection of articles. Those by Denton, Holt and Maddicott are particularly relevant.

E. B. Fryde and E. Miller (eds.), *Historical Studies of the English Parliament, Vol. I, Origins to 1399* (Cambridge: Cambridge University Press, 1970) – collection of reprinted classic articles.

J. C. Holt, *The Northerners: a study in the reign of King John* (Oxford: Clarendon Press, 1961) – influential and significant study.

J. C. Holt, *Magna Carta* (Cambridge: Cambridge University Press, 1965) – the best book on the subject.

J. R. Maddicott, 'Magna Carta and the Local Community 1215–1259', *Past and Present* cii (1984), pp. 25–65 – challenging and important interpretation.

S. K. Mitchell, *Taxation in Medieval England* (New Haven: Yale University Press, 1951) – major posthumous work.

R. C. Palmer, *The County Courts of Medieval England 1150–1350* (Princeton, N.J.: Princeton University Press, 1982) – the only modern study of the county court.

F. M. Powicke, *King Henry III and the Lord Edward*, 2 vols. (Oxford: Clarendon Press, 1947) – important, somewhat rambling.

F. M. Powicke, *The Thirteenth Century 1216–1307* (second ed., Oxford: Clarendon Press, 1962) – perhaps not satisfactory as a textbook, but full of good things.

M. C. Prestwich, *War, Politics and Finance under Edward I* (London: Faber & Faber, 1972) – more on war and finance than on politics.

M. C. Prestwich, *Edward I* (London: Methuen, 1988) – long biography.

S. Reynolds, *Kingdoms and Communities in Western Europe, 900–1300* (Oxford: Clarendon Press, 1984) – interesting new emphasis on the concept of the community, in a wide context.

H. W. Ridgeway, 'Foreign Favourites and Henry III's Problems of Patronage, 1247–1258', *English Historical Review*, civ (1989), 590–610 – one of several important articles by this author: see also his contributions to Coss and Lloyd (eds.), *Thirteenth Century England*.

G. O. Sayles, *The King's Parliament of England* (London: Arnold, 1975) – brief, important statement of a controversial position.

R. C. Stacey, *Politics, Policy and Finance under Henry III, 1216–1245*

(Oxford: Clarendon Press, 1987) – major revision of Henry iii's early years.

R. F. Treharne, *The Baronial Plan of Reform, 1258–1263* (second ed., Manchester: Manchester University Press, 1971) – now dated, but still the fullest account.

W. L. Warren, *The Governance of Norman and Angevin England, 1086–1272* (London: Edward Arnold, 1987) – Valuable modern study of the institutions of government.

S. L. Waugh, 'Tenure to Contract: lordship and clientage in thirteenth-century England', *English Historical Review*, ci (1986), 811–39. Reassessment of relations between lords and their followers.

B. Wilkinson, *Constitutional History of Medieval England 1216–1399*, vol. i (London: Longmans, 1948) – useful discussion, with documents, of individual crises.

GLOSSARY

Advowson   Right of presentation to a church living such as a vicarage

Banneret   Knight entitled to carry a square banner; a military rank above an ordinary knight

Benefice   A church living

Cahorsin   Inhabitant of Cahors in France, commonly applied to those engaged in moneylending

Carucage   Tax assessed on ploughlands

Chancery   The chief secretarial department of the government, responsible for sending out orders under the great seal

Chevauchée   Mounted raid in wartime

Curiales   Courtiers

Demesne   Land held by a lord or the king in person, not granted out; hence 'royal demesne' for crown lands

Distraint   Seizure of goods or property, usually as a means of enforcing judgement

Enfeoffment   Act of granting someone land to be held by feudal tenure

Escheat   Land which has reverted to the feudal lord from a tenant, as when the latter dies without an heir

Exchequer   The main financial department of the government

Eyre   A circuit by royal justices

Familiares   Close associates, courtiers

Farm   Annual sum payable, either in rent, or by an official such as a sheriff

Fief   Land held in feudal tenure, on condition of performing homage and service to a lord

167

Franchise A legal immunity; a delegated right to exercise jurisdiction

Honour A substantial feudal estate

Hundred A subdivision of a county

Indenture Contract drawn up in two halves, cut along an indented line, each party keeping one

Justiciar The most important office in government after the king himself, the chief political and judicial post. Vacant from 1234 to 1258, and abolished from 1265

Knight's fee A landholding traditionally owing the feudal military service of one knight

Librate Land valued in £ *per annum*. Thus a twenty librate holding was worth £20 p.a.

Lusignans Family of the counts of La Marche in Poitou: related to the English royal family through the second marriage of Isabella, King John's queen, to Count Hugh

Maltolt An excessive customs duty

March, marches Border area, as in Welsh March

Mark A sum of money, worth two-thirds of a pound (13 *s.* 4 *d.*)

Mesnie Following or retinue

Palatinate A region of considerable autonomy, such as Durham, where the lord exercised rights of jurisdiction equivalent to those the king exercised elsewhere

Poitevin Someone from Poitou in France

Prise, prises Royal right to seize goods or foodstuffs for the royal household or the army

Reeve Local official who administered a manor or small estate

Relief Feudal due paid to the lord on inheriting or taking over an estate

Retinue A lord's following

Savoyard Someone from Savoy, a county straddling the southern Alps

Scutage Money payment in lieu of feudal service

Sergeant A mounted soldier, armed much as a knight, but lacking his status and paid half as much

Sheriff The royal official placed in charge of a county

Tallage An arbitrary tax levied on towns and royal estates

Tenant-in-chief A man who held his lands directly from the crown, not from a lesser lord

Vill Village, township

Wapentake A subdivision of a county in the old Danelaw region of eastern England, the equivalent of a hundred elsewhere

Glossary

Wardrobe The main financial department of the royal household

Wardship The right of a feudal lord to rights of guardianship over the under-age heir of a deceased tenant

Writ Sealed royal order, sent either open (patent), or closed (close)

INDEX

Index

Boniface of Savoy, archbishop of
Canterbury (*d*.1270), 65, 68–9,
85, 90
Bouvines, battle of (1214), 5, 95, 98
Brackley (Northants), 35, 86, 131–2
Bracton, 21, 53
Braose, William de, 82
Braybooke, Henry de, 83
Bray, Henry de, 126
Breauté, Fawkes de, 83
Brittany, John of, earl of Richmond
(*d*.1334), 31, 90
Briwerre, William, 56
Brus, Peter de, 60
Bucuinte, Henry de, 37
Burgh, Hubert de, earl of Kent
(*d*.1243), 6, 24, 31, 51, 83, 93
Burnell, Robert, bishop of Bath
and Wells (*d*.1292), 68
Bury St Edmunds (Suff.), 50, 62
buzones, 53–4

Cahorsins, 92
Cambridgeshire, 50, 53
Canterbury
archbishops of, *see* Abingdon;
Boniface of Savoy; Langton,
Stephen; Pecham; Winchelsey
archbishopric of, 65, 84
Cathedral, 75
Cantilupe, Thomas, bishop of
Hereford (*d*.1282), 65, 70–1,
77
Cantilupe, Walter, bishop of
Worcester (*d*.1266), 65, 71–2
Carpenter, D. A., 8, 80, 87
Carta mercatoria, 126
carucage, *see* taxation
Castile, 6, 19, 98, 115
Chaceporc, Peter, 85
chancellor, 12, 24, 135; *see also*
Burnell; Cantilupe, Thomas;
Neville
Charter of the Forest, 23, 57
Chenduit family, 62
Cheshire, 33, 52, 56
Chester
earldom of, 30, 32
earl of, *see* Blundeville; Edward;
Scot

Chichester, bishop of, *see* Berksted
Cigogne, Engelard de, 82–3
Cinque Ports, 60, 133
Clanchy, M., 80, 131
Clare
Gilbert de, earl of Gloucester
(*d*.1295), 7, 25, 33, 44, 89, 106,
123
Richard de, earl of Gloucester
(*d*.1262), 34, 40, 43–4, 48, 86–
7, 131, 136
Clement iv, pope, 67, 73
Clement v, pope, 26, 68
Clifford, Roger, 40
Clericis Laicos, 74–5, 77, 121
common pleas, 135
Commons, *see* parliament
commune, 131–3, 136, 144–5, 148
of England, 60, 131
of the middling people, 60
community, 117, 129–33, 138–9,
143
of England, 129, 132, 138
of the land, 2, 22, 129–30, 137,
139, 141
of the realm, 2, 60, 123–4, 128–9,
132–4, 136–7, 139–40, 143–4,
147, 149
Confirmatio Cartarum, 7, 26, 75, 99,
122, 125, 129, 137
contracts, military, 97, 107
Cornwall, 56, 101
earldom of, 30
earls of, *see* Edmund; Gaveston;
Richard
coronation
charter, Henry i's, 66
oath, 138
council
great, 16, 134–5
king's, 8, 23–4, 59, 133–4, 136,
144
of fifteen, 6, 24
of nine, 7, 25
county
communities, 4, 6, 49–60, 62, 140
courts, 49, 52–5, 58–9, 61
Courtenay, Hugh de, 32
Coventry and Lichfield, bishop of,
see Langton, Walter
crown lands, *see* royal demesne

Index

Gascony, 1–2, 19, 73, 81, 110, 115,
    118, 120
  expeditions to, 6, 13, 42, 98–9,
    107, 124, 144
Gaveston, Piers, earl of Cornwall
    (d.1312), 8, 27, 31, 41, 82, 91,
    138
Gloucester
  earldom of, 33
  earls of, see Clare
Gloucestershire, 50, 54, 83
Grandson, Otto de, 79, 90
Great Cause, 139
Great Seal, 24, 130
Grey, John de, 65
grievances, clerical, 69–70
Grosseteste, Robert, bishop of
    Lincoln (d.1253), 17, 65, 69–
    70, 84, 149
Guala, papal legate, 67

Harriss, G. L., 109, 115–16
Hastings, Henry de, 34
Hautein, Theobald, 55
Haye, Nicolaa de la, 33
Henry II, king of England (1154–
    89), 1, 32, 36, 45, 76, 100–1,
    110
Henry III, king of England (1216–
    72)
  character, 11
  concept of kingship, 14–16, 27,
    75, 81, 136, 146
  court, 9, 18, 79, 84, 103
  local government, 56, 61
  minority, 5, 22–3, 45, 72, 83, 95
  opposition to, 17, 23–5, 38–9, 44,
    68–9, 72, 79, 87–8, 136
  personal rule, 6, 84–7, 98, 111,
    115–20, 130
  policy towards magnates, 31–3,
    42
Hereford, 65, 71, 84
  bishop of, see Aigueblanche;
    Cantilupe
Heyndon, Gilbert de, 37
Holt, J. C., 140
Hommet, William de, 37
Honorius III, pope, 72
household, 99, 103, 106
  administration, 9, 14, 83, 85, 107

knights, 90, 103, 105
Humby, Hugh of, 55
Hundred Rolls, 25, 61
Huntingdon, earldom of, 30
Huntingdonshire, 50, 52

indentures of retainer, 37, 40, 107
infantry, 107
inflation, 3, 36, 96, 110–11
Inkpen, Roger, 35
Innocent III, pope, 65–7, 75, 77
Innocent IV, pope, 17, 67, 131
interdict, 65, 119
Ireland, 1, 30, 68, 82, 90, 97, 101,
    111
Isabella of Angoulême, 85
Italian merchants, 125
  see also Frescobaldi; Riccardi

Jerusalem, kingdom of, 18, 131
Jews, 48, 61–2, 82, 91–2, 111–12,
    117–18, 120–1
John, king of England (1199–1216)
  character of his rule, 4–5, 11, 13,
    16, 51, 68, 91, 112–13, 125
  church, 65–6, 77, 119
  his bed, 44
  loss of Normandy, 95, 110
  opposition to, 38–9, 41, 61, 72,
    97, 108, 140
  patronage, 82
  policy towards magnates, 2, 4–5,
    13, 16, 18, 22, 42–3
  see also Magna Carta
Joneby, Ivo de, 37
justiciar, 22, 135
  see also Bigod, Hugh; Burgh;
    Despenser; Roches

Keighley, Henry, 14, 123, 143
Kenilworth, Dictum of (1266), 77
Kent, 50, 52
Kent
  earldom of, 30
  earl of, see Burgh
Kilwardby, Robert, archbishop of
    Canterbury (res.1278), 65
Kirkby, John, bishop of Ely
    (d.1290), 68

173

Index

Stubbs, W., bishop of Oxford (d.1901) 19, 29, 49
Stuteville, Nicholas de, 38, 42
Surrey, earls of, see Warenne
Sussex, 50, 57, 59–60

tails, English possession of, 80
taxation, 3, 9, 20, 26, 56–7, 59, 80, 109–28, 134, 141–2, 144
  of clergy, 14, 69, 74, 76, 119–20
  of Jews, 92
  refusal of, 57
taxes
  carucage, 112–13, 115
  customs duties, 111, 123–7, 137
  13th (1207), 16, 18, 112–13
  15th (1225), 126
  40th (1232), 114, 119, 130
  30th (1237), 116, 124, 130
  20th (1270), 120, 141
  30th (1283), 121
  15th (1290), 92, 120–1
  10th and 6th (1294), 120, 123
  8th (1297), 121, 138
  9th (1297), 57, 121
  20th (1300), 122
  15th (1301), 122
  20th and 30th (1306), 122
  20th (1307), 124
  25th (1309), 124
  feudal aids, 18, 22, 48, 110, 112–13, 115, 118, 122–3, 139
  Saladin tithe, 112
  tallage, 91, 112, 119–20
Testa, William, 93
Tewkesbury chronicle, 43, 87, 89
Thomas, earl of Lancaster (d.1322), 32–3
tournaments, 4, 41, 86, 131–2
treasurer, 12, 135
  see also Langton
Treharne, R. F., 87, 131
Trokelowe, John, 88
twelve, the baronial (1258), 43, 136
Twenge, Robert, 93
twenty-five barons, see Magna Carta

universitas, 129, 131, 133
universities, 64
Unknown Charter, 97–8

Valence
  Aymer de, bishop of Winchester (d.1260), 65, 68, 87
  William, bishop-elect of, 84
  Valence, William de, earl of Pembroke (d.1296), 85–6, 90, 137
Vaux, Robert de, 13
Vernon, Richard, 56
Vesci
  Eustace de, 38, 97
  Isabella de, 91

Wales, 1, 6, 30, 101, 111
  wars in, 7, 16, 26, 43, 81, 87, 96, 99, 101, 104, 134
wardrobe, 68, 83, 85, 124
Warenne earls of Surrey, 30
Warwick
  earldom of, 34
  earl of, see Beauchamp; Mauduit
Warwickshire, 50, 53
Welsh March, 38–9
Wendover, Roger, 66
Westminster, 69, 75, 119, 121, 137
  Abbey, 15, 79, 111
Winchelsey, Robert, archbishop of Canterbury (d.1313), 57, 68, 73–5, 77–8
Winchester
  bishop of, see Roches; Valence
  bishopric of, 84–5
  earldom of, 30
  earl of, see Quincy
  see also statutes
wool, 14, 125, 127
Worcester, 60, 65, 70
  bishop of, see Cantilupe
Worcestershire, 50, 57

Yarmouth, Hugh of, 75
York, 104
  archbishop of, 65, 70

177